table of contents

This collection of texts was first printed on June 24th, 2016 for the Reimagining America gathering in Kimberton, Pennsylvania taking place on July 8th-10th, 2016 (70 copies), and for the Thoreau College Prelude in Viroqua, Wisconsin on July 18th to August 5th, 2016 (24 copies). This is the second edition of the book, uploaded the next day with a few revisions, such as further examples and dates of mystery events (such as the Adamite Mysteries) and additional samples of Allied Ways.

Free culture statement: This book is not copyrighted or trademarked.

other books by the author

These books are available as free PDF downloads at https://sites.google.com/site/threefoldnow/the-books. Softcover editions can be purchased at CreateSpace.com and Amazon Europe.

▼ **The Idea—Trudging the way from a national-security state to the birth of a Second America**
(**Threefold Now, Volume One**. First printing: May 25th, 2014.)

▼ **World Wide Trisecting—Traversing from the nation-state system to a World United in truth, beauty, and goodness**
(**Threefold Now, Volume Two**. First printing: May 25th, 2014.)

▼ **Solving Burning Conflicts—Through the separation of culture and state**
(**Threefold Now, Volume Three**. First printing as a hand-stitched edition for the "Prospects for a Free Culture" gathering in Philmont, N.Y., September 7th, 2014.)

▼ **Names and Flags—Saving and renewing each and every human community through the separation and co-ordination of business, state, and culture**
(**Threefold Now, Volume Four**. First printing: February 7th, 2015.)

▼ upcoming book: **Nations and States (Threefold Now, Volume Five**). Preview maps are viewable at www.patreon.com/henryt

D1733718

We turn to you
In our distress of soul and spirit...
With the will, which we
Seek to empower
For the work at the end of the century.

—Ludwig Polzer

remarks on the introduction of a spiritual empire into the first half of the twenty-first century

by Travis Henry, June 24th, 2016[1]

Table of Contents:

I hear a lot of talk about devotion to Rudolf Steiner, Michaël, and Christ. It is sometimes too much for me.

Here's why. According to my own understanding and experience of humane wisdom (anthroposophy), what Rudolf Steiner, the Times, and the Author of the World ask for is nothing less than that each true anthroposophist would become willing to do what is necessary to put a Threefold Republic on the map of humanity's world, in this very century. Isn't that what devotion looks like?

My hope is that the very act of reading the statements in this article may contribute toward a steeling. I'm aware that concreteness is often met with all sorts of amazingly flexible, sophistic excuses. Over the years, I have already heard many of them. I welcome any reader to contact me with doubts, concerns, interest, or enthusiasm (traversetravis@gmail.com); and unless I'm unexpectedly detained by other matters, I will respond to you.

The Culmination?
Stephen Usher, a friend and mentor of mine, has written an article which summarizes some of Rudolf Steiner's statements on the prophesied culmination of the anthroposophic movement at the end of last century and the beginning of our century. The article is available at the website of the Anthroposophical Society in America:
www.anthroposophy.org/articles/article-detail/remarks-on-the-culmination-at-the-end-of-the-20th-century-952

---

[1] This article was first presented during an open conversation of the Anthroposophic Society in the Berkshire-Taconic Area on March 25th, 2016, and then published in *Deepening Anthroposophy* newsletter, issue 5.1, dated May 25th, 2016. As a living text, it has been continually revised. —TH

Steve poignantly voices:

"When I started my review of Steiner's predictions regarding the end of the 20th Century, my feeling was that the Culmination had failed. It was my decades long supposition that if it were to occur, it would be easy to recognize."

Which is common sense. And yet our common sense met with the depressing fact that no obvious Culmination was perceivable. We didn't recognize any dramatic Second Coming in the 1930s[2], nor any salvation of human civilization at the turn of the century. Were these prophecies nothing more than overambitious misperceptions by Rudolf Steiner? Are we supposed to be ashamed that, as anthroposophy's aftercomers, we didn't perceive and enact them? And the leading personalities remained concealed. If you will forgive my imaginary analogy: We felt like hobbits left alone on Weathertop, waiting for the return of Gandalf or Aragorn. Dark Kings have approached in the night, and we have been wounded.

Yet, to speak frankly, the conclusion of that article takes hair-splitting as far as it can go. To suggest that the goal of this crucial turning point was achieved around the year 2000 simply by the existence of a certain number of anthroposophic initiatives, as measured by a peak enrollment of members in the Society, turns the earnest intentions which were voiced and forged during the foundational years of anthroposophy into something threadbare, passive, and removed from the actual situation on the ground.

The conclusion isn't fruitful. Nor is it really congruent with the intentions of close colleagues of Rudolf Steiner such as Ludwig Polzer, who even after Steiner's death, tried to evolve the Czechoslovak nation-state into a Threefold Republic, or Ehrenfried Pfeiffer who aimed to do the same in the United States. Listen to their voices:

*"Since the lifework of Rudolf Steiner came to its sudden end, we shall have to bear his work ever more quietly, intimately, through death and **prepare ourselves for outer activity at the end of the century. Our souls have shown themselves too weak to fight for a new social order in the present.** We want to nurture spiritual wisdom **so that it can soon unite itself with the fire of enthusiasm.**"*

—Ludwig Polzer
(Boldface emphasis is added here, and throughout the other quotes in this article.)

*"Rudolf Steiner has painted the picture for us that the end of the century will be **the decisive moment for all of humanity.** Many religions, many esoteric groups tell us the same. I don't want to be in Heaven at the decisive moment. I would like to be here on Earth to witness **the turning toward the good** and contribute as much ego-consciousness to it as I have been able to attain."*

—E.E. Pfeiffer

Does the tone and content of Steve's offering really capture and embody such intentions?

I acknowledge that Steve offers his thoughts as a tentative and open research question out of his own wrestling with this matter, as one of our best fighters. Steve does good work for anthroposophy and for humanity, but my perspective is that the article falls short.

However, the article is a good expression of the disappointment many of us experienced when nothing spectacular happened at the societal scale by the end of the century. For me, the article itself serves as a kind of culmination, or a springboard. Where there is an ending, there can be a beginning.

The Cosmic Intelligence?

To be fair to Steve, the bulk of his article is devoted not to the question of whether the Culmination occurred, but rather to a battle for what Rudolf Steiner calls the Cosmic Intelligence, the Pan-Intelligence, or the Primal Thoughts. When I

---

[2] Beyond the usual near-death experiences and visions, which, though of deep personal significance, are, from a systemic perspective, still embryonic, since they have not yet embodied themselves in any purposeful social body, and are often unreplicable and untransmittable, and thus float above human agency. But a balance of intelligent human agency and receptivity to the divine power will be necessary in order to step up to the spiritual world's aims for this century. I hold my own view about where to look for the primary wellsprings of the Second Coming, and how these could be tapped to fuel a movement for the Threefold Republic, but it would take another article of this size to explain myself, so we'll leave it here for now.

recently asked Steve about this he responded: *"If Michaël has full command of the Intelligence then the Primal Thoughts—referenced in Steiner's work* Towards Social Renewal[3]*—will take* **outward form** *and, I believe* **one aspect of that would be Threefolding.*"

Good. That's what the rest of my article is about.

The Primal Thoughts won't open a window by themselves. Without the Cosmic Intelligence, we can't. Without us, the Cosmic Intelligence won't.

Rudolf Steiner and the Threefold Republic

One statement by Pfeiffer conveys the place that Rudolf Steiner holds the Threefold Idea within the arc of his own life's work:

"When Rudolf Steiner developed the Threefold Idea (regarding society) it seemed to him to be **the crowning achievement of his lifetime**. *He felt that in it* **the principles of the Philosophy of Freedom became fruitful for every human being** *living with every other human being. Here Rudolf Steiner was least understood. I remember one of the final discussions, which seemed hopeless and fruitless. He walked away from the table and said: 'I think I cannot go on with this work anymore; and I will devote all my time to developing in human beings better thoughts...'"*

If that was all he said, it would be a pleasing quote for those who are sure that the Threefold Republic is a dusty, broken heirloom. Yet this is how the quote ends:

"...so that they will be able later better to understand the Threefold Republic.'"

—E.E. Pfeiffer

(The words "Threefold Order" are here refreshed as "Threefold Republic.")

After the first efforts[4] for a Threefold Republic failed, Rudolf Steiner then devoted himself to offering the capacities for personal renewal and for cultural and economic initiative, for this reason: so that at the end of the 20th century and beginning of the 21st century, there would be at least a core of human beings who could now understand the Threefold Idea, and who had taken it to heart so deeply that we would be willing to do whatever harm-free but vigorous actions it takes—within the bounds our own free whim—to put a Threefold Republic on the map of the world. It may be noted that the 21st century mission is seeded into the very title of the Threefold basic text: what has been rather blandly re-titled as *Towards Social Renewal* by the U.K. and U.S. publishers, was originally titled *The Seed Points of the Social Question in Life's Necessities of the Present **and Future***. The future is now, the 21st century. There is one person who has not given up on the Threefold Republic, and *never* will:

"I believe that the world may very soon be ready for such things. I would, therefore, **never** *tire of repeating over and over again that which I believe would hasten the advancement of humanity to maturity."*

---

[3] From Chapter Three: *"It is necessary today to perceive that it is only possible to arrive at factual judgments through a return to **the primal thoughts** which are the basis for all social institutions.*

*"If adequate sources are not present from which the forces that reside in these **primal thoughts** constantly flow into the social organism, then the institutions take on forms which inhibit rather than further life. **The primal thoughts** live on, more or less unconsciously, in the human instinctive impulses however, while fully conscious thoughts lead to error and create hindrances to life. These **primal thoughts**, which manifest themselves chaotically in a life inhibiting world, are what underlie, openly or disguised, the revolutionary convulsions of the social organism. These convulsions will not occur once the social organism is structured in such a way that the tendency is prevalent to observe at what point institutions diverge from the forms indicated by **the primal thoughts**, and to counteract such divergences before they become dangerously powerful.*

*"In our times, divergences from the conditions required by **the primal thoughts** have become great in many aspects of human life. The living impulse of **these thoughts** stands in human souls as a vocal criticism, through events, of the form the social organism has assumed during the last centuries. Good will is therefore necessary in order to **turn energetically to the primal thoughts** and not to underestimate how damaging it is, especially today, to banish them from life as 'impractical' generalities."*

[4] Attempts were made to establish a Threefold Republic in Austria-Hungary, in Germany, in Switzerland, and in the contested German-Polish border province of Upper Silesia.

From "Social Threefolding" to the Threefold Republic

The phrases "social threefolding" and "threefold social organism" lend themselves to the most flexible and vague interpretations. Yet flexibility is a quality which is balanced by the quality of firmness. That is why, throughout this article, the original German phrase of "three-membering the social organism" and its various English renderings ("Threefold Commonwealth", "Threefold Order", and so forth) are replaced with "Threefold Republic"—a firm designation which was used by Ralph Courtney who pioneered the anthroposophic center in Spring Valley.[6] Likewise, the adjective and verb "threefold(ing)" are sometimes refreshed here as "trisected" and "trisecting."

The Threefold Republic is simply what humane wisdom has to offer in the field of political science and statecraft. The term "social threefolding" is often confused with "associative economics", but the economy is only one-third of a Threefold Republic. The Threefold Republic is nothing less than the transformation of a national state into three sovereign commonwealths, or republics[7]: an Economic Republic comprising the entire economy, a Rights Republic as a streamlined, humanized political state which holds no culture-shaping powers, and a Cultural Republic as a sovereign third sector. The Economic Republic and the Cultural Republic are not governments. Each business enterprise and cultural initiative is viewed as a kind of micro-republic.[8] Whereas the Rights Republic is composed of *citizens*, the Economic Republic is composed of millions of cooperative, entrepreneurial micro-republics, while the Cultural Republic is composed of millions of free cultural micro-republics. The coalescence of these two distinct sectoral associations provides humanity with a palpable, visible experience that the economy is not the government, the government is not the economy, and that a truly libertarian culture follows the tune of neither state control nor monied power.

What a Waldorf school or biodynamic farm is to a "school" and a "farm", the Threefold Republic is to a "country." "Social organism" is Rudolf Steiner's refreshed synonym for "a country."[9] So a "Threefold Social Organism" is nothing less than a trisected *country*—a trifold evolution of an entire nation-state.

The Threefold Republic does not yet exist

Maybe it goes without saying, but there are no Threefold Republics yet on earth. In a similar way, there were no Democratic Republics on earth[10] prior to the foundation of the American Republic and French Republic in 1776 and 1792. The Democratic Republic didn't just magically happen. Human beings got sick and tired of groaning under inherited, controloholic imperial monarchies. Individuals and groups came to understand the Democratic Republic idea. We desired it and enacted it. The window to the Democratic Republic was opened by human comprehension and willingness.

---

[5] Only GA numbers are referenced throughout this article, to lessen the possibility of wriggling out of engaging with the words in a fresh way. Otherwise, the tendency is to say: "Oh, I've read that lecture, and so have thousands of other anthroposophists. It's already covered." If a more exact citation is needed, there is a GA reference list appended to this article.

[6] For example, the 1950 newspaper article: "Ralph Courtney Lectures For Polit[ical Association] About **Threefold Republic**" from the *Vassar Chronicle: Vol. VIII, No. 6, p. 5*, the student newspaper of Vassar College, Poughkeepsie, New York, November 4, 1950. It's reprinted here: https://sites.google.com/site/threefoldnow/vassar

[7] Historically, the word *commonwealth* (meaning "public well-being") was simply an Anglicization of the Latin phrase *res publica*, meaning "public matter." "Commonwealth" and "republic" are essentially synonyms.

[8] For example, in regard to a school: *"The school, therefore, will have its own administration run on a **republican basis** and will not be governed from above. In a true **republic of teachers** we will not have things to fall back on comfortably in the form of directions from the principal's office, but we must infuse our work—infuse ourselves—with what gives each one of us full responsibility for what we need to do."* —Rudolf St., GA 293

[9] See, for example: *"The social goals described here, although valid for humanity in general, can be realized by each individual **social organism** regardless of **other countries'** initial attitudes"* (GA 23). This sentence, and the rest of the Threefold basic texts, simply make no sense if "social organism" is interpreted to mean a single school, farm, curative community, or philosophical society.

[10] Sticklers will note that in the 1700s there were a few proto-democratic, proto-republican pockets in Switzerland, the Netherlands, Corsica, northern Italy, and among indigenous peoples off the edge of the imperial maps. But unlike the Democratic Idea and the Republican Idea, which originate in Athens and Rome, the Threefold Idea is a new idea which has no historical precedent.

Now we are groaning under the Democratic Republic...the "Twofold Republic." What was once a blessing has passed its acme, and is lingering beyond its time. On the other hand, there is no question of reverting to an atavistic, authoritarian "Onefold Republic" founded on state socialism or cultural fundamentalism. The only way is to move onward. Yes, there were social "threenesses" in humanity's past—the three Manuvian castes of ancient India, the three classes in Plato's *Republic*, the three council fires of the indigenous Anishinaabe alliance in the Great Lakes region of North America, the three estates of medieval Europe, the tripartite message of the Great Peacemaker of the Haudenosaunee (Iroquois) League, the triarticulate motto of the French national government, and the three branches of the American national government—but a national community's differentiation into three sovereign, territorially-overlapping republics, operating out of three distinct principles, and with every person holding a dignified, participatory role in each of the three republics—has never yet existed on the face of the earth.

A Waldorf school is an actual brick-and-mortar school. A biodynamic farm is an actual farm, on a particular patch of land. There was no Waldorf school on earth prior to 1919, and no biodynamic farm before 1926.[11] Likewise, a Threefold Republic would be an actual country which has unfolded itself into three sovereign and independent sectors, each with their own formative principle, their own leadership, deliberative forum, administrative nexus, embassy network and intersocietal relations, and flag.[12] It isn't so much of a "Threefold Republic", but *three republics*—the three commonwealths are united only in that each individual human being within that territory is a member of all three, and that there is a coordinative Threefold Senate which serves as a treaty-based interface for the everyday relationship between the three republics.

Big things, big scale, big thoughts
In regard to turning the tide of human history, little community-sized "beacons of light" will not be enough.

*"It is a question, not of little things, but of **big things** [...] From any measures on a small scale, one can truly no longer hope for much today. Today we should after all be learning to see, that at the bottom **nothing is to be accomplished except by treating things on a big scale**, as I might say."*

—Rudolf St., GA337

A relatively dense network of anthroposophic initiatives in a region doesn't "count" as a country. It just won't cut it. I have lived and worked in various anthroposophic centers in North America, such as the Threefold Community in Spring Valley near New York City, and the anthroposophic node in Columbia County, in Upstate New York, centered on Hawthorne Valley Association and the four surrounding Camphill communities. We are doing good work, yet the formative force of these two nodes pales next to even a county government, state school board, or municipal zoning board.

It is as if we have been stirring a pint-sized little bucket of biodynamic preps to apply to a single tomato plant in our window, when what is asked for, and what humanity needs, is a working farm with full-size, production-capable greenhouses.

*"Little thoughts will get us nowhere, so we must **pluck up the courage to think big thoughts**."*

—Rudolf St., GA194/196

The very existence of a Threefold Republic on the map will change the course of world history. All eyes will turn to the Threefold Idea when it stands on the stage of the world. This will be front page news in all countries, including Russia and the Arab Lands—branches of humanity which are semi-consciously allergic to the nation-state system.

---

[11] The Loverendale farm in the Netherlands, managed by Pfeiffer, is credited as the world's first BD farm. Though the BD toolbox had been laid out in 1924 via the Agriculture Course, there was a two-year lag time before implementation. Similarly, the Threefold Republic toolbox was laid out in 1917 via the Trisecting basic texts, but as of now, there has been a 99-year lag time (so far) prior to implementation.

[12] For a list of structure features conveyed by Rudolf Steiner, see "Details of a Threefold Republic" compiled by the author. https://sites.google.com/site/threefoldnow/details

The Michaëlic Republic: a Demand, a Thought, a Force, a Power, an Aim, a Prophecy, an Impulse, a Mission, a Will, an Action, and a Path

Steve offers the question: if the Culmination has already happened, then what is the role of anthroposophy for the remainder of Michaël's reign? The article suggests these activities: collating Rudolf Steiner's œuvre, fighting off any attempt of Catholics, Mormons, and New Agers to distort his legacy, and imparting his corpus of writings to academia.

I am not the only one who finds those to be a sad and underwhelming set of goals for the People of the Defender God.

In contrast, someone else voices a more vigorous goal:

*"[The Guardian Michaël] demands of humanity as a whole: Separate what has up to now been interwoven in a chaotic unity in the State idol; **separate this into a Spiritual Life, an Equity State, and an Economic State** [...] **otherwise there is no progress possible for humanity**."*

—Rudolf St., GA202

Lectures are often glossed over in an impersonal, easily dismissible way. How does it sound to refresh the words?:

"O human being...follow me. To each and every one of you who are representatives of humanity and of humane wisdom, I say: to follow me is to join together in trudging an inner and outer path which will truly culminate in a triform society in this generation, first at a country-sized scale, and then globally."

I hear the word "Michaëlic" thrown flexibly around as if it meant "everything nice and progressive." Yet *the* Michaël Thought is something very specific and concrete:

*"One would venture to say that when we speak of **the Threefold Republic impulse, the campaign was a test to see whether Michaëlic Thought has grown strong enough** to enable one to feel how such an impulse flows forth directly from the formative forces of time. **It tested whether Michaëlic Thought has grown strong enough in enough individuals.** And the results were negative. **Michaëlic Thought** is not strong enough in even a small number of individuals to be felt in the wholeness of **its time-shaping force and power**."*

—Rudolf St., GA 223

An impulse flowing directly from the formative forces of time? Time-shaping force? Powerful words. For Michaël, the only victory is to vigorously yet peaceably evolve all 193 nation-states into 193 Threefold Republics. That victory begins with putting one Threefold Republic on the map, and culminates with the replacement of the United Nations Organization with the Trisected Societies Organism. Ita Wegman voices this task:

*"A task is still awaiting fulfillment: [...] the forming of humanity into a **true and worthy social body over the whole earth**. **Michaël's aim** is to bring about that **true knowledge and understanding of Christ** which, living itself out in **moral action**, leads [...] the **world in its totality** to harmony."*

—Ita Wegman, <u>On the Work of Michaël</u>, 1930

In Rudolf Steiner's last address, one moment he is speaking...

"Those who are anthroposophists today in the true sense will feel a strong urge to come down again to the earth very soon..."

...and then he begins to prophesy...

*"...And with a faculty of **prophecy connected with the Michaël Impulse**..."*

...and then The Archangel speaks, in the Fighter's own words, spoken from the core of the Sun, through the tongue, teeth, and lips of a human mouth, who says...

*...It can be foreseen that many anthroposophic souls will come again to the earth at the end of the 20th century **in order to bring to full realization** the anthroposophic movement which must now be established on a firm and sure foundation."*

*"**Every anthroposophist** should be moved by this knowledge: "I have in me the impulse of anthroposophy. I recognize it as the **Michaël Impulse**. I wait and am strengthened in my waiting by true activity in anthroposophy at the present time **in order that** after the short interval allotted in the 20th century to anthroposophic souls between death and a new birth, I **may come again at the end of the century** to promote the Movement with **much more spiritual power**. I am preparing for the new age leading from the 20th into **the 21st century."***

It may be noted that the 21st century is included in the Prophecy. We come at the end of the 20th century. Here we are. And we enact a new civilization in the 21st. The prophecy continues...

*"**If you all** [...] are able [...] to **make the Michaël Thought live in your deeds in all its strength and all its power**—if this is so, **then will you be true servants of the Michaël Thought**, worthy helpers of **what has now to enter earth-evolution** through anthroposophy, and take its place there in the meaning of Michaël."*

*"Because this is so, my dear friends, I have made the effort today to rise up and speak to you [...] May the words so speak to your soul that you **receive the Michaël Thought** in the sense of what a faithful follower of Michaël may feel when, clothed in the light rays of the Sun, **Michaël appears** and points us to **that which must now take place**."*

If we do that, *then* we will be true servants of Michaël. "Michaëlic" is an "if, then" quality.

And so, except when speaking with children[13], I would refrain from using the word "Michaëlic" to refer to any kind of courage other than becoming willing to begin to conceive and organize, and to follow through to completion, a full-blown Threefold Republic on one country-sized patch of earth. That is the outward turning point of human civilization. There is no better representation of the fruits of humane wisdom than that.

"Those who love peace must learn to organize as effectively as those who love war."

—MLK paraphrased

Who is like Michaël?
When I expressed this recently, one anthroposophist asked me these questions:

Q: *"Travis, aren't you overstating your point a bit here? Do you really mean to say that any use of the term "Michaëlic" is invalid unless it refers to creating a Threefold Republic? That would mean that much of anthroposophy is not Michaëlic."*

Yes and no.

Yes. That is exactly what I'm saying. Any pathway which doesn't explicitly, consciously, and volitionally lead to a Threefold Republic in our generation, is not Michaëlic. It is Luciferian. Nearly all of anthroposophy and "social threefolding", as it currently exists, has fallen into a left-hand path.

And no—Of course, nearly all of the anthroposophic content is potentially relevant to the upcoming Michaëlic Republic.

Speaking honestly of myself, I simply did not bear the inner resources and circumstances necessary to invent the Threefold Idea or anthroposophy myself. We stand on the shoulders of giants. Study, comprehension, and self-education are complementary to meditative work. Therefore, those who preserve the legacy of Rudolf Steiner's textual output, or who

---

[13] Rudolf Steiner even asked that teenagers be taught the details of a Threefold Republic:

"In the seventh and eighth grades, you could give them what is in <u>The Seed Points of the Social Question</u> [a.k.a. <u>Towards Social Renewal</u>]."

—p68, <u>Faculty Meetings with Rudolf Steiner</u>, SteinerBooks, 1998.

Waldorf students are explicitly taught anthroposophic dance, so why not explicitly teach anthroposophic political science and statecraft?

work toward deepened and clarified methods of cognition, are indirectly preparing for societal trisecting. We first need to be able to tell our "left from our right" before we are able to perceive the threefold potential which is confusedly, harmfully packed into our current social structure. Anthroposophy works in a precursorial way in further fields, such as by providing a vibrant space for children to grow up as nuanced persons, or by producing exquisite, farm-fresh food to strengthen us. This is vital, necessary, preparatory work. And...these are not a Threefold Republic.

Anyone who is truly awake to our societal reality would eventually feel the burning necessity of a full-fledged Threefold Republic, in this very generation. How ethical is an ethical individualism which has nothing to say or do about the national-security state? I would rather not see a repeat of anthroposophy's bowing and scraping display toward the nation-state beast in 1935.[14]

Q: *"In your view, was Rudolf Steiner's whole life non-Michaëlic other than the threefolding content? And any of your colleagues who are not working on the Threefold question would also not be Michaëlic."*

Rudolf Steiner was working Michaëlically through most of his life, because most everything (but not everything) he did was semi-consciously (prior to 1917)[15] or consciously (from 1917 through his death in 1925) preparatory for clearing a path whereby societal trisecting would reveal itself as necessary to wide swathes of humanity.

I'm not here to open cans of worms. Yet here we go: Rudolf Steiner is not the Archangel Michaël and is not God. As far as I know, no one, not even Rudolf Steiner, wears a permanent "Michaëlic" merit badge. "Michaëlic" is an aim, an action, and a result. If you need a word for initiatives which semi-consciously (but not yet fully consciously) prepare for a Threefold Republic—such as most Waldorf schools and Camphill communities—these could be named "preparatorial" or "proto-Michaëlic." That definitely sounds better than Luciferian. Of course anthroposophic initiatives are relatively health-bringing in their particular fields of life; but will they somehow magically lead to a Threefold Republic on their current trajectory? No they won't. Not without the formation of a plan and a willingness for implementation. To the extent that the Threefold Republic goal is not really digested and understood, and is not really planned for in this generation, these proto-Michaëlic initiatives are bent.

Anthroposophy without the Threefold Republic cannot help but be Luciferian, because there is an unspoken assumption that the sphere of statecraft, and the scale of a country, cannot be penetrated by a higher power.

*"This work is: to let the Michaël Power and the Michaël Will **penetrate the whole of life.** The Michaël Power and the Michaël Will are none other than the Christ Will and the Christ Power, going before in order to implant in the right way into the Earth the Power of the Christ."*
—Rudolf St., GA238

Q: *"And aren't all the other initiates and leaders of humanity non-Michaëlic, because they have not explicitly worked toward threefolding?"*

Without the Threefold concepts, even the most well-intentioned, god-fueled person and initiative will eventually fall to corporatism or governmentalism. Mahatma Gandhi received a copy of the Threefold basic text from Walter Johannes Stein. If he had read, understood, and enacted certain provisions[16], several million human lives would have been spared.

---

[14] "Letter to Adolph Hitler from the Anthroposophical Society", November 17, 1935.

The letter is reprinted in *The Development of Anthroposophy Since Rudolf Steiner's Death* by T. H. Meyer, SteinerBooks, 2014.

[15] In 1917, Rudolf Steiner first conceived/perceived the Threefold Human Organism in March, and in May-June he worked through the details of the Trisected Societal Organism with Otto Lerchenfeld and Ludwig Polzer.

[16] Such as the full differentiation between national culture and political governance, described in Chapter Four of *The Seed Points of the Social Question*. Their fusion, even in Gandhi's mind, resulted in the Partition of India into a Muslim Pakistani nation-state and a secular Indian nation-state, with concomitant nationality-based massacres and displacements. Westerners naturally view the secular nation-state as the "good guy"; yet civic nation-building is still an expression of state-based culture formation.

The Threefold Republic is what the genuine spirit of our time calls for and leads toward. Other times had their own crucial goals. The human leadership of past centuries did not have the foundation to conceive and enact the Threefold Idea. We do.

Besides "proto-Michaëlic" another term I find helpful is "Dismasic"...referring to Dismas the Thief, who was crucified on the left-hand side of the hill of Golgotha. During the unfolding of the event, Dismas began to make amends for his mistaken concepts and actions, and in light of this he is now known in Christian tradition as Saint Dismas the Good Thief. In my experience of the Occupy Movement, its crypto-Marxian substance was, at its best, poignantly Dismasic. Much of the Cultural Creative movement is presently Dismasic, in the sense that it leans toward the Social Democratic idea of liberal/progressive governmentalization—what Nicanor Perlas refers to as R.U.S.T.: Residual Unresolved Statist Tendencies. Whether these Dismasic-leaning persons and initiatives ally with the Michaël Path remains to be seen. One thing's for sure: our Dismasic fellowmen are not going to join a path which does not yet exist. Once we have started clearing the way, then we will see whether our efforts evoke an evolution beyond Luciferianism and Dismasism. And for us, the very action of clearing the path will evolve our own anthroposophic impulses from proto-Michaëlism to ultra-Michaëlism.

When, later in this century, we are standing on the steps of the Threefold Senate, in a Threefold Republic, and the beauty of humane wisdom permeates nearly all of the organizations and corporations therein, then I myself would concede to acknowledging all human beings who contributed to that fruition as *Michaëlic.*

From that echelon, the next task will be to evoke a Threefold Republic in each and every one of the other 192 nation-state boxes which have locked down humanity's world. And for the grand finale: to tri-fold the United Nations System.

Q: *"Especially, aren't his lectures on the 'Mission of Michaël' non-Michaëlic also, because they don't explicitly advocate threefolding?"*

Well, let's look at those lectures. As usual, Rudolf Steiner says a lot, about a lot of things. And yet, there is also this:

*"In describing this to you, I am describing to you at the same time **the deepest impulses of the social question.** For the abstract League of Nations [now, the United Nations] will not solve the international problem. Such abstractions do not **bring the people together all over the earth.** But the spirits who lead the human beings into the super-sensible, and of whom we have spoken during these days, **will bring people together.** Externally, humankind approaches today serious battles. In regard to these serious battles which are only at their beginning—I have often mentioned it here—and which will lead the old impulses of earth evolution ad absurdum, **there are no political, economical, or spiritual remedies to be taken from the pharmacy of past historical evolution.** [...] This leading ad absurdum of human evolution can be **counteracted only** by that which leads human beings on the path toward the spiritual: **the Michaël Path** which finds its continuation in the Christ Path."*

—Rudolf St., GA194

I implore the reader to not doze off into fuzzy warmth by the end of that paragraph. Could the reader please practice reading between the lines in a more concrete way than is usually expected, and to hold back from saying: *"Oh the Michaël Path toward the spiritual?...I've got it covered. I'm a Waldorf graduate (or parent or teacher), an anthroposophist, and a member of the Christian Community. Check!"*

If you want to find anthroposophists who will smile and nod and agree that Michaël is surely flexible about his[17] thoughts and aims, then you don't have to look far—at this point, there are probably 60,000 of them. Yet I am one person who is saying and (sometimes) doing something different. This whole article is voicing the assertion that though are many preparatorial, proto-Michaëlic thoughts and initiatives, there is only one *Michaël Thought*...one single-minded *Michaël Aim.*

---

[17] Michaël and other trans-physical beings, could just as well be referred to by either gender.

My perspective is that the pathway will entail the formation of an actual fellowship of fiercely individuated human beings, of all stripes and walks of life, of any and all religions and creeds, which through a shared, anthroposophically-enhanced initiatory experience, become more close-knit, harmonious, and genuinely loyal to each other, and to their shared ideal, than any tribe, or movement, or society, or knighthood has ever been, and whose explicit goal is to pervade all of external life with humane wisdom, and to implant a Threefold Republic on the map of the world. From that geographic bridgehead or foothold, personal and civilizational renewal will be propagated across the earth.

*"The real impulse of [the true social organism] consists in the realization of siblinghood in the widest sense of the term in the **external structure of society.** [...] One must first understand what is meant by siblinghood. On the physical plane **the present state-systems must be replaced throughout the whole world by institutions or organizations which are imbued with siblinghood.**"*

—Rudolf St., GA185 (The word "brotherhood" is here refreshed as "siblinghood.")

The Threefold Republic resides entirely in the human will
*"Having said really a great deal here, which was thrown to the winds, which never made its way into people's heads at all [...] What is wanted now, would be to set to work and **actually propagate the Threefold Idea, as it is.** Of course there are any number of things in the way of this; **but they all reside entirely in the human will.**"*

—Rudolf St., GA337

It is possible to put a Threefold Republic on the map. Other ideas have led to organizations which pioneered new states. For instance, the idea and goal of the Zionist Movement was to put a Jewish nation-state on the map of the world. Within a few decades, this was realized through human will. From the time Theodor Herzl wrote *The Jewish State* pamphlet in 1896 to the political independence of the Israeli nation-state in 1948 was only 52 years...less than one life span. And as I write this in early 2016, an Islamicist State has recently erupted out of the exhaustion of the nation-state idea in the Arab World, also through human will.

Is it possible for similarly concrete results to be reached through a concerted human will which wields only humane, transparent, harm-free, but vigorous methods and soul force? I wonder if Rudolf Steiner ever asked for such a concrete goal in regard to humane wisdom. Did he ever ask this of any circle?

The Threefold Republic is the only true salvation of humanity
Steve suggests that the scattered sum of the existing anthroposophical organizations at the turn of the century was all that was necessary to save humanity:

"The full list of individual and group initiatives could be summed—like the cobblers' spare leather scraps that were used by Vidar to destroy the Fenris wolf—and if the sum is sufficient, then one could state that the conditions necessary for a culmination had occurred."

I suggest that the preparatory, spare leather scraps we have gathered *will* be enough to begin the task of our century, but that *there will be no Vidar to use them* to feed and redeem the Wolf unless we form ourselves into a Vidar-shaped republic. Nothing else will end the lingering nightmare and deflect humanity's descent into an upward trajectory.

*"Humanity will have no say in matters **if it cannot arrange its social organism in a trisected way.** This is what will **have to be regarded as the only healing, the true salvation of humanity.**"*

—Rudolf St., GA296

Nothing else but putting at least one full-blown Threefold Republic on the political map will stop the catastrophic intrusions, societal inequities and distress, and the ongoing confinement of the human being by the interests of national security.

*"Either one must deign to **submit one's thinking to the demands of reality,** or nothing will have been learned from the débâcle, and this self-inflicted misery will be **endlessly** perpetuated and compounded."*

—Rudolf St., GA24

We don't get to skip this test. Christopher Budd puts it this way:

*"Whether the external forces of 'law and order' prevail over the inner ordering power of such ideas as Rudolf Steiner would have us take up, remains to be seen. The choice between the two will not, however, be a new development in history, but will mark **the return of the very same problem** that arose with World War I, but which we baulked at and shied away from."*

—C.H. Budd, *Rudolf Steiner, Economist: An Introduction,* 2012

Recovering from denial of the Threefold Idea

What do our American fellows think will save their national community? Prayers and meditation? Good thoughts from anthroposophists? No. Haven't we neared the point in the story where the only genuine fruit of prayer and meditation and esoteric study will be the willingness to supersede the nation-state system and pioneer a fully-articulated Threefold Republic, somewhere on this wide Earth?

To put it frankly: in regard to the goal of this century, why are the sons and daughters of humane wisdom, who otherwise embody such integrity in their chosen fields, so spacey, disorganized, and ignorant of what is possible in the field of anthroposophically-extended statecraft? Those who know me know I have those and other character defects as well, so I am not condemning anyone. We are doing good work, and that is nothing to be ashamed of. Heaven knows I'm not up to the task...I forget appointments, I hate public speaking, and I make lots of mistakes. Yet at least one person in earth is now clearly voicing what was, and still is, intended for the 21st century.

What underlies such denial of the Michaël Thought...a denial which is so strong that it blocks even grasping what a Threefold Republic really is? Why, in the past 90 years has no one voiced what I am voicing today? How can so many immerse themselves in the details of Christology or other facets of humane wisdom, yet fall asleep when approaching the Threefold Idea? Admittedly, Rudolf Steiner's basic texts on societal trisecting could hardly be written in a more boring and abstruse way, I am sorry to say. Nevertheless, our century is a good time to awaken with some serious energy and enthusiasm.

"One can do nothing with people who do not want the Threefold Republic, but only with those who are filled with the idea."

—Rudolf St., GA24

Though all sorts of small-scale, healing initiatives such as Waldorf schools, biodynamic farms, anthroposophic arts, and Camphill communities do, or could, contribute towards making a space for this, in the end, when we look back from the perspective of the 22nd century, anything less than a full-blown Threefold Republic will have been a failing. We won't fail though.

Question: "What will the 21st century bring?"
*Karl König: "I have the impression that **the new social order will begin in the 21st century**."*

—Karl König, "The Threefold Social Order" talk given in Scotland, 1964

The United States and the Threefold Republic

Here are some statements on the possibility and necessity of initiating a Threefold Republic in America:

*"Rudolf Steiner once said, "If one wants to erect a Threefold Republic, **the American Constitution could be used as a model of a constitution of such a republic.** [...] I remember I stood there myself during those discussions about what he called the American Constitution of Washington [...] He always said, "**The Constitution of Washington could be the basis upon which we now could build the Threefold Republic**, if we could only find **one territory on earth which is willing to accept it**."*

—E.E. Pfeiffer

Please be clear that the U.S. Constitution, as it exists, could only serve as a solid but bare foundation. A Threefold Republic would require three constitutional amendments which articulate the separation of economy, state, and culture (especially education). Frankly, any and all of the other 192 national constitutions could be, and will need to be, likewise amended.

*"The English-American world may gain world dominion; but **without the Threefold Republic** it will, through this dominion, pour out cultural death and cultural illness over the whole earth."*

—Rudolf St., GA194

Cultural death results from commercialization and governmentalization of the cultural wellsprings. Preventing cultural death from pouring out over the whole earth sounds like a job for the legitimate leadership of humankind.

*"Well, the actual victor is the Being of the English-American Peoples, and as a result of forces that I have often described here, this Being of the English-American Peoples is destined to dominate the world in the future. [...] The transfer of external dominion will take place with the relentlessness of a force of nature. **The resulting responsibility, however, will be of deep significance for those souls.** Already inscribed in the book of human destiny is the question: **Will there be a sufficient number** among those impelled to assume external dominion, as though by a force from outside, **who feel a responsibility for inserting into this entirely external, materialistic dominion**—for that is what it will be, make no mistake—**an impetus for spiritual life**?"*

—Rudolf St., GA194

"Those souls" are the anthroposophists, and other human beings of goodwill, who are now ensouled as daughters and sons of Hengist and Horsa[18], and of General Washington. The responsibility is to insert a Threefold Republic into the Anglo-Saxon global empire, and thereby sheathe the bloody sword.

*"I have spoken about something quite terrible: about the platitude. But if the world had not become so platitude oriented, there would be no room for the **introduction of a spiritual empire**. Precisely because everything old has now become platitudes, a space has come into being in which **the spiritual empire can enter**. Especially in the West, **in the English-American world** people will continue to speak in the usual terminology, things that come from the past. It will continue to roll on like a bowling ball. It will roll on in the words. You can find innumerable expressions especially in the West which have lost all meaning, but are still used. But not only in these expressions, but in everything described by the old words the empty platitude lives, in which there is no reality, for it has been squeezed out. **That is where the spiritual, which has nothing of the old in it, can find room.** The old must first become empty platitude, everything that continues to roll on in speech thrown overboard, and **something completely new must enter**, which can only propagate as a world of the spirit.*

*"Only then can there be **a kingdom of Christ on earth**."*

—Rudolf St., GA196
(In these quotes, the words "Anglo-American" are refreshed as "English-American.")

If that were all he said, the flexibly-minded would surely interpret "spiritual empire" to be an analogy, to be realized through personal development, and through just continuing to grow our existing cultural and economic initiatives. But no, he is talking about nothing less than a full-blown Threefold Republic:

*"When we realize that we are living in the kingdom of platitudes under which only economic imperialism glimmers—then will we call for the spirit, invisible but real. We will call for a knowledge of the spirit, one which speaks of an invisible kingdom, a kingdom which is not of this world, in which **the Christ-impulse can actually gain a foothold. This <u>can only happen</u>** when the social order is tripartite, threefold: The economy is self-administered, the political state is no longer the absolute, all-encompassing entity, but is exclusively concerned with rights alone, and spiritual [cultural/educational] life is truly free, **meaning that here in reality a free spiritual [cultural] sector can be organized.**"*

---

[18] *"This British being originally arose from the Angles and Saxons who had the occult sagas of Hengist and Horsa when they migrated over towards the British Isles."* —"<u>Things in Past and Present in the Spirit of Man</u>", Lecture 3, March 28, 1916, Dornach, GA 167. The English-speaking empire began in the year 449 A.D., with the words *Nemet oure Saxas!* ("Take out our swords!"), whereupon the Celtic leadership of Britain was opportunistically assassinated at a peace gathering. You could look it up. It's not a pretty story, and lingers as an undercurrent in our will and character, as English-speaking peoples. The millennium-and-a-half of instinctual political-economic opportunism calls for a complete karmic reversal.

*"**It's an either/or situation:** Either efforts remain exclusively oriented towards the economy—in which case the fall of earthly civilization is the inevitable result—or spirit will be poured into this economic empire, in which case **what was intended for earthly evolution will be achieved.** I would like to say: Every morning we should bear this in mind very seriously and **all activities should be organized according to this impulse.**"*

—Rudolf St., GA196

Turning "this economic empire"—the United States and its global economic institutions—into a humane, wise Threefold Empire is the authentic Christ Impulse of our century. There are few instances where Rudolf Steiner describes only an either/or choice. This choice is between America and reality. The United States is the Roman Empire of our day, which is "taxing" the whole world. Yet from a higher perspective, it is but a petty, half-witted human organization which is standing in the way.

One might venture that Michaël is a persona who is much larger than, and unafraid of, the United States Government and other national-state beasts, unafraid of their security services, and unafraid of the oligarchic economic powers which wield the National Law as tools to unlawfully shape humanity. Yet that would be a mistaken view. It is said that even Michaël himself is afraid of this conglomeration of material power[19]—and yet he chooses to stay on course despite his fear. This needs to be done. If even Michaël is afraid, then who does he and we need to become like? The Father? The Ground of the World? Michaël is practicing becoming like that, like an Archë, who stands on new ground, superseding the unitary state.

Do you think that this lecture given from a hill in Switzerland was intended to only evoke the will of the few American anthroposophists who were living in the 1920s? Of course not. These words are a message to all those souls—Manichæan heretics and true anthroposophists from all nationalities—who would soon be dropping down into North America and the English-dominated world at the end of the century. Such a gigantic task is beyond the means of any one human being, and Rudolf Steiner himself spoke of "four times twelve" persons who would arise to do what is necessary. The words are a message to himself and to the four times twelve human leaders who will arise to put a Threefold Republic on the map in this 21st century.

*"If, in the near future, **in four times twelve human beings, the Michaël Thought becomes fully alive**—four times twelve human beings, that is, who are recognized not by themselves but by the Leadership of the Goetheanum in Dornach—**if in four times twelve such human beings, leaders arise** having the mood of soul that belongs to the Michaël festival, **then** we can look up to the light that through the Michaël Stream and **the Michaël Activity will be shed abroad in the future among humanity.**"*

—Rudolf Steiner's last address

In regard to leadership in the 21st century, there is specific mention of Novalis. Pfeiffer also reports statements from Rudolf Steiner about the individual known as Mani, which are included as an appendix to my article. My perspective is that it is worthwhile to learn to think like Rudolf Steiner or Novalis or Mani. What would these Great Ones do if they found themselves in our spot, at this moment, in our century?

Jesus Christ and the Threefold Republic
The preceding statements about America refer to the Threefold Republic as the *Foothold of the Christ Impulse*, the *Kingdom of Christ on earth,* and the *Spiritual Empire.* The knowledge and will to bring about the Threefold Republic is the permeation of our being by the Representative of Humanity.[20]

---

[19] *"Michaël, who has the degree of an archangel, does not have the rank of Satan, who has the degree of an archë. Michaël is 'only' an archangel. From Michaël's point of view Satan is not a power to be despised but a power to be immensely feared, for Michaël sees this power who belongs to the hierarchy of the archai as being more exalted than himself. Michaël, however, has chosen to go in the direction that is the same as that of earth evolution."*
—<u>The Book of Revelation and the Work of the Priest</u>, Lecture 11, September 14, 1924, Dornach, GA 346.

[20] To my non-Christian-identifying cohorts: Don't worry, lest we be tripped by names, the Higher Power of humane wisdom and of the Threefold Republic is not boxed in by Christian terminology. The true Yeshua had a hand in founding all religions and philosophies (including secularism). Would He not be willing to be clothed again in their conceptual and aesthetic raiment? For more, see "My Politics and Religion Article in LILIPOH Magazine" and "A Pluri-religious Movement for Renewal":
(The footnote continues on the next page.)

"Just as the shepherds in the field and the Magi from the East went after the proclamation to see how that which was to bring humanity forward appeared as a little child, so must modern humanity make our way to Initiation Science in order to **perceive, in the form of a little child, what must be done for the future by the Threefold Republic** *based on Spiritual Science.* **If the old form of the state is not trisected** *it will have to burst—and burst in such a way that it would develop on the one side a wholly chaotic spiritual [ideological] life, completely mephistophelean and luciferian in character, and on the other side an economic life again luciferian-mephistophelean in character. And both the one and the other would drag the state in rags after them. In the East there will take place the development more of mephistophelean-luciferian spiritual [ideological] states; in the West there will be the development more of mephistophelean-luciferian economic life—if humanity does not realize* **through the permeation of our being by Christ** *how we can avoid this, how* **out of our knowledge and out of our will** *we can proceed to bring about* **the trisecting** *of what is striving to separate. This will be* **human knowledge permeated by Christ**; *it will be* **human willing permeated by Christ**...*"*

—Rudolf St., GA202

("Ahrimanic" is here refreshed as "mephistophelean." "Orient" is refreshed as "East."
The East includes the Middle East, neo-statist Russia, and the North Side of Korea.)

The Nation-State: a Desolating Idol, Abomination, Demon, and Dragon

In contrast, the fused cultural-economic state (the "unitary state") is named an "idol." The quote continues...

"...And it [human knowledge and willing permeated by Christ] will express itself in **no other way** *than that* **the idol of the Unitary State will be trisected.***"*

—Rudolf St., GA202

Who among us relishes resisting or superseding the U.S. government, its tax collectors, school inspectors, zoning officers, and security services? Or any of the other 192 national governments, for that matter. The nation-state and its National Law are what entrances humankind to the point of bloodletting and controloholism—of what Rudolf Steiner refers to as "political alcoholism" (GA143).

The practice of peaceably standing taller than one of these is an experience of standing up to a god of ancient times.

The idol is spoken of again in Rudolf Steiner's last address before he died:

"If this Michaël Power is able verily to overcome all that is of **the demon and the dragon** *(and you will know what that is) [...] then will you be true servants of the Michaël Thought"*

The demon and the dragon is the idol of the nation-state, which is standing where it should not be. In the gospels, Jesus names this:

*"***The SHIKUTS MESHOMEM ["abomination that causes desolation"]*** *spoken of by the prophet Daniel, standing in the holy place where it should not be (let the one reading this, take heed)"*

—Matthew 24:15 and Mark 13:14

The mixed national-economic-state is standing in the way of further individuation. It is standing in the way of authenticity, beauty, and goodwill. Global corporations and their purchased national governments have bent the spine of humanity, and have placed a cap or lid on our uprightness. The left-hand powers compel nearly all human children to be raised in government agencies ("public schools"), while the right-hand powers subject humanity to an "unquestionable" Darwinian economic ideology, where much of waking life is spent toiling to make rent and keep the wolf from the door. The experience of these two systemic hindrances can desolating and devastating...it presses out the soul, and calls forth personal affliction or conformity, resulting in cold cities, redneck countrysides, and ticky-tacky suburbs filled with wounded representatives of humanity.

---

www.patreon.com/posts/my-politics-and-5373999
https://sites.google.com/site/4religiousrenewal

Geographically, this desolating nation-state-economic idol covers the entire earth, except for Antarctica and the high seas. And this fixed idea of a nation-based state and state-formed nation is standing especially strongly at the midmost crossroads of humanity, in the holy place from which emanated the first turning point.

We shall not fail. Our courage will not fade.

It will take a miracle of willingness, yet we will do it. We will not fail. The same "impossibility" was encountered when Theodor Herzl voiced the idea of a Jewish State, but it was accomplished. The tenacity of our Jewish fellowmen is a quality to admire and emulate. Yet the means and fruits of the Michaëlic State will truly be in service to all of humanity, in a way that a national state cannot be.

Both Rudolf Steiner and Michaël himself say it will be so:

*"Michaël insists, as I have told you, that **his dominion shall prevail and penetrate at any cost.**"*

—Rudolf St., GA237

*"After you have gone through the gate of death, you will find in the spiritual supersensible worlds [...] all those with whom **you are to prepare the work <u>that shall</u> be accomplished at the end of the century, and <u>that shall</u> lead humanity past the great crisis in which it is involved.**"*

—Rudolf Steiner's last address

Prophecies don't just "happen." Wouldn't it be nice if we could sit by and let the Holy Comforter and the higher power of our guardian angels do it for us? Good prophecies exist to be understood and enacted. Windows are made to be opened.

The will of the Spiritual World...that is the Loving God, and all that is holy and beautiful and worthwhile...is couched behind the words of Rudolf Steiner's last address. This century calls for the maturity of humanity—beginning, perhaps, with anthroposophic humanity. This is possible. Not only is it possible, it will happen. Won't we do it? I ask this of myself too, because there are sometimes any number of things I would rather do than step up to the Threefold Republic. Lest the prospect of penetrating the State through civil resistance and elections seem too daunting, I offer that pioneering a model, parallel, symbolic (but not *merely* symbolic) Threefold Republic Project, similar to the existing Free State Project in New Hampshire, would be an avenue for living into the idea in a way that is fast, free, and fun.

Another doorway into the idea would be through artistic-fictive portrayals of a near-future Threefold Republic, imbued with lovingly crafted, picturesque detail and mythopoeic charm.[21]

Everyone who is reading this came into the Earth sphere at or about the end of the 20th century. We are still at the beginning of the 21st century. Not even a quarter of the century has passed. If we set our mind and will to it, a lot can be done by 2050. My perspective is that the Century of Nightmare ends not simply by semi-consciously passing a certain numerical date on the calendar, but moreso when we actually begin to intentionally clear a path for the Threefold Republic. That's when *Our Century* begins. Anthroposophic nostalgists may say of the 1920s: "those were the days." But for us *these are the days*. When will the daughters and sons of humane wisdom take up the harm-free sword of Spiritual Empire?

Though Steve quotes from the little book *Rudolf Steiner's Millennium Prophecies* by Heinz Schoeffler, there is one piece of important information which did not make it into Steve's article:

---

[21] The Threefold Idea is briefly voiced in Shirley Latessa's *Auragole Quartet* stories which take place in the fantastic setting of the Deep Earth: *"If I can once again unite the west, I will call into being a council duly elected by the people. It will be its task to protect the rights of every single citizen. I will also bring together a group of men and women who are knowledgeable in trade and commerce. Their task will be to see that no one in the west goes without. And third, I will give free reign to all creative people, those gifted in the various arts or spiritual pursuits."*

—spoken by Auragole, in *Auragole and the Last Battle*, Lindesfarne Books, Great Barrington, Massachusetts, 2005. Sadly, the soon-to-be realized Threefold Republic is not (yet) depicted in the existing volumes.

Also, *The Working of the Spirit*, the upcoming Mystery Drama by Michael Burton and Marke Levene, touches on the Threefold Republic idea.

*"The Threefold Republic is completely done for in this century. It cannot become a reality. It will again be possible at **the beginning of the coming century** when a window of the spiritual world will open **in order to make it possible**."*

—Rudolf St.

***

appendix: three weird concerns of the threefold republic

Mephistopheles Enfleshed and the Threefold Republic

I will mention three especially "occult" (esoteric/hidden) aspects which would "weird out" some audiences, but which are relevant to the goal of a Threefold Republic in the 21st century. Besides the more obvious need for a separation of monied power from human rights and personal development, the Threefold Republic at a country-sized scale is a prerequisite for three esoteric events, which I mention here only in passing to show that the Threefold Republic is a concrete, necessary thing upon which other events will follow.

The first occult concern is that a Threefold Republic is necessary to be able to deftly respond to the enfleshment of Material Power.

"...if the old Unitary State as such—whether a democracy, a republic or a monarchy—does not become trisected, this is simply a way of helping Mephistopheles' incarnation."

—Rudolf St., GA191

*"People nowadays flee the truth, and one cannot give it to them in an unvarnished form because they would ridicule it and scoff and jeer. But **if one gives it to them through the Threefold Republic as one now tries to do, then they will not have it either**—not the majority, at any rate. **The fact that people reject these things is just one of the means which the mephistophelean powers can use and which will give Mephistopheles the greatest possible following** when he appears in human form on earth. This disregard of **the weightiest truths** is precisely what will build Mephistopheles the best bridge to the success of his incarnation."*

—Rudolf St., GA193

In these quotes, "Ahriman" is freshly rendered as "Mephistopheles." An even better description of "Ahriman" is "the personal experience of being boxed in and locked down by outer corporatist and governmental hindrances." Who among us hasn't experienced and felt this formative force?

I would rather not hear talk about the incarnation of Mephistopheles/Ahriman from anyone who is not willing to initiate or join a society or fellowship whose explicit singular purpose is to put a Threefold Republic on the map in this century.

Mechanical Occultism and the Threefold Republic

The second occult concern is that the existence of a few Threefold Republics is a prerequisite for developing a new, moral form of energy which will have the strength of nuclear power with the cleanliness of solar power.

"The 'West-people' of England and North America will develop the material-mechanical occultism. They will be able to create machines, mechanical devices which work with hardly any human effort; which work with the help of the 'Laws of Sympathetic Vibrations'. These machines will do about 90% of the work, and all the social and material trouble of work as we know it now, will cease to exist."

—Summary of Rudolf St.'s words, GA186
(Summarized by Wim A. M. Leys of the Netherlands.)

The work-saving implications of this kind of energy are hinted at the Mystery Dramas:

"No longer will men be forced to dream away their existence, plant-like and in an undignified manner, on narrow factory floors. Technological forces will be distributed in such a way that everyone will be able to comfortably use and determine what he needs for his work, in his own home."

But there is a downside to such a power:

*"The possibility will thus come about of rendering unnecessary nine-tenths of the work of individuals within the regions of the English-speaking peoples. Mechanistic occultism will not only render it possible to do without nine-tenths of the labor still performed at present by human hands, **but will give the possibility also of paralyzing every uprising attempted** by the then dissatisfied masses of humanity."*

—Rudolf St., GA186

Frankly, if living energy were revealed now, the American people would use it to annihilate our self-made enemies. And the technology would be scooped up by the immortal corporate beings and gilded family lineages. That power would be used to further lock down most of humankind into sheepish, consumer-shaped boxes.

So when would it be healthy and fruitful for these kinds of devices to be discovered and utilized? Ehrenfried Pfeiffer, who worked professionally as a scientist in the field of etheric forces, asked Rudolf Steiner himself:

*"I asked when will the time be ready? Answer: **when the social conditions are such that no misuse of this force can be done for selfish purposes;** that would **only be the case** if the Threefold Republic would be practiced at least over a few territories on earth. Until this time, experiments in the direction of using the etheric forces would not be successful or should not be done."*

—E.E. Pfeiffer

*"I once discussed with Rudolf Steiner the question of **when would be the proper time for the application of etheric forces for technical uses.** He said that this would be **when the Threefold Republic is established**."*

—E.E. Pfeiffer

How were Pfeiffer's aspirations reflected in the will of the anthroposophic community?

*"Since especially the Anthroposophical Society has never **put the social problem in front of all its aims** [...] I see no other way but to bury the instructions with regard to the use of the etheric force deep down in my chest."*

—E.E. Pfeiffer

Mani and the Threefold Republic

A third occult concern is the need to form a country-sized space for human individualities to arrive and unfold without being mucked up. Instead of a school- and family-sized pocket of light, the salutary influence is expanded into a country-sized emanation. In this regard, the individuality who initiated the Manichæan Impulse is singled out:

"Until there is a Threefold Republic the size of Württemberg, Mani cannot or will not incarnate."

—An unconfirmed indication of Rudolf Steiner which I have heard expressed verbally more than once.

Württemberg is a former State of Germany, with a then population of 2.4 million (similar to the U.S. state of Kansas) and an area of 7,500 square miles (similar to the U.S. states of New Jersey or Connecticut).

Pfeiffer and Bernard Lievegoed elaborate on Mani's connection with the Threefold Republic:

*"We see that from now on, **Mani will be connected with the social order, with the questions of a proper social order for human beings.** [...] The Threefold Republic of Rudolf Steiner is particularly a preparatory work to bring about a future incarnation of Mani. [...] He said that Mani could not find a suitable body yet, that all the forces he would be able to bring to an incarnation would be destroyed by modern education." [...]*

*"Therefore he said that Waldorf education needed first to come into being and that the Threefold Republic must also come into being. Therefore **I would see it as our immediate task to bring about this Threefold Republic first through thought and then through action,** so that Mani can incarnate. By karma, Mani's incarnation would be due by the end of the [20th]*

*century. Whether this will be possible I do not know, but if the Threefold Republic and Waldorf education were established he could incarnate. I see it as our task to make the preparations so that he can incarnate again. **Such an incarnation would bring about a complete change of trend in history. People fool around with things like the United Nations** and don't know how to solve world problems. [...] The followers of Mani who were incarnated as heretics in the 12-13th centuries, are to prepare for the end of the century. [...] Mani **will take over in the next century** as the spiritual leader of humanity."*

—E.E. Pfeiffer

"Rudolf Steiner once said to Pfeiffer that he had started the Waldorf school and the Threefold Republic to make the incarnation of Mani and his helpers possible. Let us hope there are enough active anthroposophists to accomplish what Mani needs for his development. And let us hope anthroposophists will recognize him once he is here."

—Bernard Lievegoed
(In these quotes, "Manu" and "Manes" are rendered as "Mani.")

Manichæans were fierce, yet luminously peaceable heretics, who boldly followed their star regardless of hindrances, and regardless of what others thought of them.

According to the anthroposophic legendry, the individuality of Mani returned to earth as Percival, the grail knight. Would not the Grail Republic be a fitting outward quest of Percival and his knightly peers? Why not become like that? We can all be Manis, Novalises, Co-Founders, and Initiates. We are the Great Ones we've been looking for.

Now where is the pathway that leads from here to there?

***

Travis Henry
Harlemville, N.Y., USA
traversetravis@gmail.com
Patreon site: "Travis H. is creating Books and Civilizational Renewal": www.patreon.com/henryt
Threefold Now—Movement for the Differentiation of Economy, State, and Culture:
https://sites.google.com/site/threefoldnow/home

References:

▼ *"We turn to you in our distress..."*: p.515, *Ludwig Polzer-Hoditz: A European* by T.H. Meyer, Temple Lodge, 2014.
▼ *"Since the lifework of Rudolf Steiner came to its sudden end..."*: p.515, ibid.
▼ *"Rudolf Steiner has painted the picture for us that the end of the century..."*: quote featured on the back cover of *Ehrenfried Pfeiffer: A Modern Quest for the Spirit*, by Thomas Meyer, Mercury Press, Spring Valley, N.Y., 2010.
▼ *"When Rudolf Steiner developed the Threefold Idea..."*: p.6, Lecture 1, August 1, 1947, given at Threefold Farm in Spring Valley, N.Y., printed in *Rudolf Steiner: Two Lectures by E.E. Pfeiffer*, Vulcan Books, Spring Valley?, 1979?
▼ *"I believe that the world may very soon be ready for such things..."*: "National and International Life in the Threefold Social Organism", *The Social Future,* Lecture 6, October 30, 1919, Zurich, GA 332a.
▼ *"The social goals described here, although valid..."* "International Relations between Social Organisms", Chapter Four, *The Seed Points of the Social Question* (a.k.a. *Towards Social Renewal*), 1919.
▼ *"The school, therefore, will have its own administration run on a republican basis..."*: "Appendix: Speech on the Evening before the Course", August 20, 1919, Stuttgart, GA 293.
▼ *"It is a question, not of little things, but of big things..."*: "On Propaganda of the Threefold Social Order", *The Threefold Order of the Body Social—Study Series II,* June 9, 1920, Stuttgart, GA 337.
▼ *"Little thoughts will get us nowhere..."*: *Ideas for a New Europe*, Lecture 6, Dornach, GA 194 and 196.
▼ *"[The Guardian Michaël] demands of humanity as a whole..."*: "The Magi and the Shepherds: The New Isis", *The Search for the new Isis the divine Sophia*, Lecture 3, December 25, 1920, Dornach, GA 202.
▼ *"One would venture to say..."*: from p.505 of *Rudolf Steiner: A Biography* by Christoph Lindenberg, SteinerBooks, 2012. The original quote is from "The Cycle of the Year as Breathing Process of the Earth" Lecture 3, April 22, 1923, Dornach, GA 223.
▼ *"Those who are anthroposophists today..."*: "The Individuality of Elias, John, Raphael, Novalis—The Last Address given by Rudolf Steiner", September 28, 1924, Dornach, GA 238.
▼ *"Those who love peace..."*: This iconic quote and meme is probably a paraphrase of a statement by Martin Luther King from a march against the war in Viet Nam, on State Street in Chicago, March 25, 1967. The original words may be: *"Those of us who love peace must organize as effectively as the war hawks."*

- ▼ *"This work is: to let the Michaël Power and the Michaël Will penetrate…"*: "The Individuality of Elias, John, Raphael, Novalis—The Last Address given by Rudolf Steiner", September 28, 1924, Dornach, GA 238.
- ▼ *"This work is: to let the Michaël Power…"*: "The Individuality of Elias, John, Raphael, Novalis—The Last Address given by Rudolf Steiner", September 28, 1924, Dornach, GA 238.
- ▼ *"In describing this to you…"*: "Michaelic Thinking", *The Mission of the Archangel Michael,* Lecture 3, November 23, 1919, GA 194.
- ▼ *"The real impulse of…"*: "The Relation Between the Deeper European Impulses and Those of the Present Day", *From Symptom to Reality in Modern History,* Lecture 9, November 3, 1918, Dornach, GA 185.
- ▼ *"Having said really a great deal here, which was thrown to the winds…"*: "On Propaganda of the Threefold Social Order", *The Threefold Order of the Body Social—Study Series II,* June 9, 1920, Stuttgart, GA 337.
- ▼ *"Humanity will have no say in matters if…"*: August 9, 1919, Dornach, GA 296.
- ▼ *"Either one must deign to submit one's thinking…"*: "An Appeal to the German People and to the Cultural World", 1919, GA 24.
- ▼ *"One can do nothing with people who do not want…"*: "Wanted: Insight!", *The Renewal of the Social Organism,* Article 20, 1921, GA 24.
- ▼ *"Rudolf Steiner once said, 'If one wants to erect…"*: pp.52-53, *Ehrenfried Pfeiffer: Notes and Lectures, Compendium II,* Mercury Press, 1991.
- ▼ *"The English-American world may gain world dominion…"*: "The Old Mysteries of Light, Space, and Earth", *The Mysteries of Light, of Space, and of the Earth,* Lecture 4, December 15, 1919, Dornach, GA 194.
- ▼ *"Well, the actual victor is the Being of the English-American Peoples…"*: December 14, 1919, Dornach, GA 194.
- ▼ *"I have spoken about something quite terrible: about the platitude…"*: "The History and Actuality of Imperialism, Lecture 1", February 20, 1920, Dornach, GA 196.
- ▼ *"When we realize that we are living in the kingdom of platitudes…"*: "The History and Actuality of Imperialism, Lecture 3", February 22, 1920, Dornach, GA 196.
- ▼ *"If, in the near future, in four times twelve human beings…"*: "The Individuality of Elias, John, Raphael, Novalis—The Last Address given by Rudolf Steiner", September 28, 1924, Dornach, GA 238.
- ▼ *"In the East there will take place…"*: "The Magi and the Shepherds: The New Isis", *The Search for the new Isis the divine Sophia,* Lecture 3, December 25, 1920, Dornach, GA 202.
- ▼ *"And it will express itself in no other way…"*: Ibid. (the same Isis lecture)
- ▼ *"political alcoholism"*: "Overcoming Nervousness", Munich, January 11, 1912, GA 143.
- ▼ *"Michaël insists, as I have told you…"*: "Entry of the Michaël Forces", *Karmic Relationships,* Volume III, Lecture 9, July 19, 1924, Dornach, GA 237.
- ▼ *"After you have gone through the gate of death…"*: "The Individuality of Elias, John, Raphael, Novalis—The Last Address given by Rudolf Steiner", September 28, 1924, Dornach, GA 238.
- ▼ *"The Threefold Republic is completely done…"*: p.36, *Rudolf Steiner's Millennium Prophecies* by Heinz Herber Schoeffler, reported from a conversation with Clara Michel, Henry Goulden Book, Cornwall, U.K., 1999.
- ▼ *"If the old Unitary State as such…"*: *The Influences of Lucifer and Ahriman,* Lecture 2, November 2, 1919, Zurich, GA 191.
- ▼ *"People nowadays flee the truth…"*: *The Ahrimanic Deception,* October 27, 1919, GA 193.
- ▼ *"The 'West-people' of England and North America…"*: summarized by Wim A. M. Leys, hosted at *The Storm's Nest* internet site administered by John Penner, accessed May 19, 2016. This is a summary of Rudolf Steiner's lecture, "The Challenge of the Future, Lecture 3", December 1, 1918, Dornach, GA 186.
- ▼ *"No longer will men be forced to dream away their existence…"*: *The Guardian of the Threshold,* Scene One, 1914, GA 14.
- ▼ *"The possibility will thus come about of rendering unnecessary nine-tenths of the work…"*: "The Challenge of the Future, Lecture 3", December 1, 1918, Dornach, GA 186.
- ▼ *"I asked: when will the time be ready?"*: p.111, "Fragments of a Biography" from *Ehrenfried Pfeiffer: A Modern Quest for the Spiritual* by Thomas Meyer, Mercury Press, 2010.
- ▼ *"I once discussed with Rudolf Steiner the question…"*: pp.41, Lecture 5, December 22, 1916, *The Task of the Archangel Michaël* by Ehrenfried Pfeiffer, Mercury Press, 1985.
- ▼ *"Since especially the Anthroposophical Society has never…"*: p.111, "Fragments of a Biography" from *Ehrenfried Pfeiffer: A Modern Quest for the Spiritual* by Thomas Meyer, Mercury Press, 2010.
- ▼ *"We see that from now on, Mani will be connected…"*: pp.41-42, Lecture 5, December 22, 1946, *The Task of the Archangel Michaël,* by Ehrenfried Pfeiffer, Mercury Press, 1985.
- ▼ *"Rudolf Steiner once said to Pfeiffer…"*: p.96, *The Battle for the Soul* by Bernard Lievegoed, Hawthorn House, 1993.

'Threefold Night' by Christopher Wetmore.

politics and religion article in LILIPOH

May 1ˢᵗ, 2016.

The editor of LILIPOH magazine asked:

"How does anthroposophy "the wisdom of the human being"—or to put it another way—how does <u>humane</u> wisdom teach us ways we can have a healthy social life while allowing people to have the freedom to hold opposing political and religious views?"

My response is published in the Spring 2016 issue, which is at newsstands now. Here's the text:

***

In America there is a tradition that in polite conversation one doesn't speak of politics or religion. Nevertheless, does humane wisdom ("anthroposophy") have anything to say about these two "impolite" subjects?

In regard to politics, humane wisdom teaches that one of the largest expressions of destructive polarity is that of the left-right divide. The right is sure that the best possible future would be to privatize everything and turn all of life into a business, while the left is just as set on "governmentalizing" everything, including education. Their clash conjures an unsavory "false middle" which is vested in maintaining the status quo.

Ultimately, humane wisdom calls for each American to learn to perceive what is behind this destructive polarity, and to recognize that both "halves" of humanity are carrying something worthwhile, though incomplete. There can be no sustainable "healthy social life" within islands surrounded by a sea of corporatism or statism. Those who have some connection with the anthroposophic way of life comprise one segment of humanity that is especially poised to be able to tell our left from our right.

We have practiced perceiving the polarities in all phenomena: growth and decay, hot and cold, curve and line, thesis and antithesis, resentment and fear. These are perceptions of what is archetypally named "Lucifer" versus "Mephistopheles" (or "Ahriman"). On a large scale, humane wisdom has this to say about what Americans in everyday life view as the "blue states" and the "red states":

"If you consider the two main categories of parties, the liberal and conservative, you know that each has its own program. When you look above to see what each is a reflection of, then you discover that ahrimanic being is projected here into the conservative views, luciferian being in the liberal thoughts. Down here, one follows a liberal or conservative program; up there, one is a follower of an ahrimanic or a luciferian being of some hierarchy. ... The moment you pass across the doorway [of clear perception or death] it becomes necessary really to understand all this clearly, and neither be fooled by words nor succumb to illusions. ... Actually he [or she] is a follower of either Lucifer or Ahriman..."

—Rudolf St., <u>Spiritual Science as a Foundation for Social Forms</u>", 1920

***

As for religion, humane wisdom teaches that all varieties of religious experience are leaves on a single tree. At the original center of each worldview is a shared higher power, who is the most advanced representative of the gods and of humankind. This central being or person been perceived by all human cultures: the Great Mystery in North America; the Tao in China; Vishnu in India; Ormazd in Persia; Osiris in Egypt; Belenus among the Celts; and Helios in Greece. This representative leaped down into physical perception and walked the earth at the fulcrum point in humanity's story.

But the doctrines of our earlier worldviews had crystallized prior to this event, and so their outer form has not yet consciously harmonized with this mystical fact. And though the three Abrahamic religions each perceive a reflection of this representative, their denominational "leaves" on the tree have often been blown one way or the other, bending their conceptions of the spiritual world to the point that the name of the representative has been misapplied to superficiality or authoritarianism—sometimes in a terribly harmful way.

Before his death in 1925, Rudolf Steiner prophesied that in the mid-1930s, the representative would appear a second time—this time as a force of life, rather than as a physical man. Humane wisdom asserts that no human being is able to approach personal renewal without connecting—through thought, desire, and action—with one's own conception of this being of love.

22

This is a new deal: the representative of humanity is willing to go by any name and to be clothed in the fabric of any worldview. In service of this "second wind," humane wisdom seeks to renew each worldview, and restore it to truth, beauty, and goodness. So far, this effort has given rise to a single communion, beautifully embodied in the Movement for Religious Renewal—a name which presently synonymous with the Christian Community.

For this humane way to fully spread its shade across the wide earth, more than one leaf will need to receive sunshine and water.

***

Travis Henry lives in Columbia County, New York. For more, you're welcome to visit his sandboxes:

▼ A Pluri-Religious Movement for Renewal: https://sites.google.com/site/4religiousrenewal
▼ Threefold Now https://sites.google.com/site/threefoldnow

my thanksgiving story

Dear friends,

Three years ago, I enjoyed Thanksgiving in the County Jail. A European friend recently asked me if I had ever recounted that story. Back in the day, I did slap together a rough webpage about those events (Quest for the Threefold Declaration)—but not a unified, coherent, chronological account. It takes me awhile to "process" and articulate life, and I'd never just written out what happened.

So I took her up on the request. The result is probably too long, and is still a pretty fragmented kaleidoscope of anecdotes, yet it serves as the fullest account of the whole experience which I could muster. You're welcome to skim through it to find any interesting passages which catch your eye. I mostly refrain from naming names of friends, since I don't want drag others into the story without permission.

If you have any questions, comments, further remembrances...or even if you just find some typos...feel free to contact me: traversetravis@gmail.com. Hopefully something in here is of use to someone. Anyway, here goes...

- ▼ **Part 1: A Threefold Declaration**
- ▼ **Part 2: The Trial**
- ▼ **Part 3: One Jail and Two Prisons**
- ▼ **Part 4: The Aftermath**
- ▼ **Takeaways**

Part One: A Threefold Declaration

It was the summer of 2012. I was, and am still, devoted to the idea of putting a Threefold Republic on the map of the world, in our century. So that in at least one country-sized patch of earth, there is a total differentiation between Business, State, and Culture.

That summer, some friends and I were studying Thoreau's "Resistance to Civil Government", which steeled my will. I was fired by these words:

"If one HONEST man, in this State of Massachusetts, ceasing to hold slaves, were actually to withdraw from this co-partnership, and be locked up in the county jail therefor, it would be the abolition of slavery in America. For it matters not how small the beginning may seem to be: what is once well done is done forever."

I felt that humanity is enslaved by the 193 "fused corporatist-governmentalist nation-state boxes"—in other words, "national governments" and the economic corporations which have purchased them. Whether I qualify as the HONEST (all caps) man or not, someone's got to step up to bat. Back in my early thirties, I had ceremonially washed my hands of co-partnership in the nation-state beast.[22] Now I felt that if I took one meaningful jail-worthy stand in the name of the Threefold Idea, then it would somehow be done forever. Even if no one knew about it, the beginning could not be erased.

I heard there was an Occupy National Gathering in Philadelphia during Independence Day weekend. The day and place where the U.S. Declaration of Independence was signed in 1776. I decided to go.

I was then only partially aligned with Occupy...I had participated in our local Occupy groups a bit, had visited the Occupy camps in Portland (Oregon), Great Barrington (Massachusetts), and Zuccotti Park (NYC), and had even co-pioneered a local

---

[22] When I lived in Sacramento, California, I visited the U.S. senator there and presented the idea of national amends. There was no significant response, so I visited again to ceremonially renounce my membership in the U.S. nation-state-as-it-exists (or any other nation-state). Then I went outside to a nearby park and asked a passerby if they were an American, and if they would witness for me: he was a Chinese-American and agreed to witness. There was a water-fountain in the shape of an indigenous bowl, and I literally washed my hands of the Americanist Way, and its global Nation-State Way.

Occupy group based in Philmont and Harlemville named "Occupy Social Threefolding." But though I value the humane effort I witnessed, Occupy's aesthetics and conceptions lean to the Left in an incomplete way. I feel it is crucial to bring along both the "right hand" and the "left hand" of humanity.

Me with some friends in Zuccotti Park back in 2011. I'm in the green hoodie on the right.
[Note for this edition: the Fellowship of Humane Way has not yet begun, so my image is not yet fully effaced.]

I wrote up a Threefold Declaration and read it to my local Occupy group—we were meeting in the Philmont Beautification, Inc. space on the corner of Main Street in Philmont; and that evening, my colleagues helped polish the text.

I printed off a stack of copies to take with me to Philadelphia. I didn't know exactly what to do with them until I got there; but I vaguely imagined dumping the stack off a balcony in Independence Hall, like the White Rose did in the atrium of the University of Munich in 1943.

From seeing pictures of the "Signing of the Declaration of Independence" as a kid—in history books and on the 2-dollar bill—I imagined there was some kind of balcony in Independence Hall:

And I had heard a legend about how a mysterious figure in the balcony had encouraged the original signers. However, once I got there, it turns out, there's no balcony in the room! Admittedly, in retrospect, there's no balcony visible in the painting either...but my imagination had filled in the top of the picture!

Also, with the sewing skills of my artist friend Nick P. (plus a Mexican woman from a nearby fabric factory who kindly volunteered to punched the grommets), I had made cloth "threefold flags", and took them with me. Here are the designs:

The Threefold States in the Homeland of the Dream

The Living Economy in the
Homeland Crowned with Goodwill

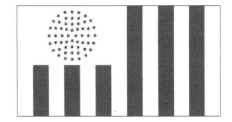

The Constitutional Governance in the
Homeland Where All Human Beings Are Created Equal

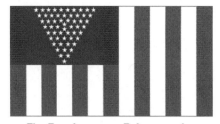

The Revolutionary Culture in the
Homeland of the Free

The 56-star patterns were calculated for Threefold Now by mathematician Skip Garibaldi from Emory University in Atlanta. As for the colors: the economic flag has a red canton with blue stripes. The cultural flag has a blue canton with red stripes (like the U.S. national flag). And the rights flag is white with half-blue, half-red stars and stripes.

Here's a photo of me with the Living Economy flag (in my house).
[Note for this edition: Humane Way hasn't begun, so I have not yet fully anonymized.]

At the ONG, I participated in various events and conversations. One highlight was that two Occupiers volunteered to carry the Rights Flag and Cultural Flag in the march (which I prefer to call a parade), while I carried the Economic Flag.

There was a Black Nationalist there who spoke of the uniqueness of Philadelphia ("Philadelphia is the only place where the U.S. police dropped a bomb on our people. A bomb!") I offered him to carry a flag. He asked me to explain the three flags, and he chose the Rights Flag, and yelled out: "Yo! We have an Occupy Governance!" Near the end of the parade, he had wrapped the flag around his shoulders like the cape of a prize fighter, and was wielding the copper flagpole in a precarious way. At that point, I retrieved them and thanked him.

The Rights flag at the Occupy National parade.

The Cultural Flag was carried by another man—when I met up with him at the end, he suggested that a triangle of stars looks like the pyramid on the back of the U.S. dollar. (On that original flag, the triangle's tip pointed up.) Some weeks later, I showed my flags at Camphill Kimberton in the countryside of Philadelphia, and a man there likewise suggested that the triangle was a symbol of ancient Egyptian hierarchy. After reflecting on the feedback from these two men, I flipped the triangle point-down (as depicted in the illustration above)—symbolizing a revolutionary "lowerarchy" where individuality is sovereign.

I don't own a camera...I found these photos on another ONG participant's facebook page. I added blue markers to point out the two flags and flagbearers.

(Most of the other photos in this story are snagged from the internet too.)

The Cultural flag.

Anyway, back to the ONG: In one small group conversation there was talk about doing *something* on such an important, symbolic date as July 4th, 2012; but no one agreed on what to do. Yet in that group I met a person who was sparking to do something. Her name is Meenal. She was/is a local Occupier from Philadelphia.[23]

Meenal (from her facebook).

---

[23] I shared this story with Meenal. Her response: *"Read it in entirety just now. I had no idea what you went through. Although I don't understand the Threefold philosophy, I fully support your efforts. Wish I could've helped you when in Philadelphia. And no, I certainly don't mind being a part of your story!"*

She helped me write a shorter Declaration using Occupy-style language:

An Occupy Declaration of Interdependence

We the people of the United States reject corporate rule and assert our economic interdependence with one another.

We move to amend our constitution to firmly establish the separation of business and state.

We stand for the transformation of our corporocratic, oligarchic economy into a humane, living economy whose primary purpose is to fulfill real human needs, such as food, clothing, and shelter.

We support those businesses and economic associations who accept what is socially just.

We value an economic system which is occupied with the human qualities of brotherhood/sisterhood, mutual aid, solidarity, co-operation, and altruism.

We are dedicated to a dignified future where human rights and human individuality are not for sale. Given the pervasiveness of the Corporate State, this constitutional change could be described as regime change in America.

On July 3rd, Meenal brought me around to various people who might help craft the declaration, and showed me another declaration which was published around that time (Derrick Jensen's "A New Declaration"), along with a pamphlet about separating Wealth and Rights through a constitutional amendment. The theme of a "Declaration of Interdependence" was in the air—there was a canvas board with that title at the Occupy camp (in the parking lot of the Quaker meeting hall); and in the park, there was a giant typewriter with an endless supply of yellow paper on which anyone would type their own Declaration of Interdependence.

I signed the board with "Occupy Social Threefolding." (This photo was from a tweet.)

Coincidentally, my own Threefold Declaration which I'd written beforehand used the word "Interdependence"—but only to refer to only the economic sector—not to the cultural sector (the legitimate place for individualistic Independence) or rights sector (the interface of Independence and Interdependence).

At that point, I was imagining going into Independence Hall with a small group and voicing our Declaration of Interdependence, and then leaving, with no arrests necessary. I talked with a few people who had participated in our group conversation, but willingness was lukewarm. Yet there were enough "maybes" for me to continue.

So as to have a better picture of the place, I "scouted" the outside of the Hall a day beforehand, and talked with the rangers (park police), and got to know them a bit. That turned into an adventure in itself. When I walked up to the entrance gate, a young security guard[24] was casually standing in the way, languidly chatting about this-and-that as I stood there waiting. I said: "excuse me", and he slowly sauntered out of the way. Then at the security check, he simply barked "Turn around!" I felt it was outrageous to greet each park visitor with such military-style service, at what is supposed to be an immersive cultural site. I said "No." He was flustered and called for backup. I didn't know what to do. An older security guard and two rangers came.

In that moment, from an ordinary perspective, it would have been better to say, "Fine, then I won't visit our Independence Hall." And walk out. Yet I stayed and tried to explain how I experienced this as rude service. Police in these times, are sometimes looking to turn a simple matter into a federal case (literally). So they questioned me, and issued a minor citation. At that point in life, I didn't know of the simple right to say: "Am I free to go? If not, then arrest me; if so, then I am leaving now." (I invented that insight for myself the next day though. This should really be taught to young people as a basic right of citizenship.) As the police were questioning me on the stoop of a building near the entrance, one of the most beautiful persons I've ever seen stopped and watched and witnessed the police talk with me. This passerby was an ordinary person who was there for a tour; yet the presence of their human beauty somehow helped me feel that I was in the right place.

So after receiving my "penalty slip", I left. I could see that the various police officers and guards had mixed views on my perspective—some were more empathetic; some were clearly antipathetic. Nevertheless, it turned out to be good to establish some human contact before finally going in.

As for the next day's action, of the various persons from our group session, one young man said he would come, and we set a time to meet in the morning. Even though he didn't show, it was actually helpful that he *said* he was coming, because I don't know if I would've gone through with it if I knew ahead of time that I'd be the *only* one. It's understandable for him or anyone to not come with me—there were a lot of other Occupy events going on that day[25], and this was early in the morning; hard to rise from a late night of tent sleeping. I also sensed that despite the fierce talk of Occupy, there was an understandable, human reluctance to really step in the heart of the matter. I overcame my reluctance.

---

[24] The security guards (employees of a private corporation) wear uniforms which mimic police uniforms (servants of the public governance)—a practice which is banned in some countries, such as the Netherlands. It says something that access to this public cultural site is administered by a private corporation who outwardly mimics the rights governance.

[25] I was planning on attending a joint-Occupy-Tea Party parade later that morning if I hadn't been snagged.

Independence Hall.

So that morning at 830, I went to the visitor center, where I picked up a "timed ticket" for the first tour at 9am. I waited at the meeting spot in case someone showed up late. The Occupy legal team had requested that they be notified of any "autarchic actions" beforehand, so I called their number and briefly stated that I was going to voice a declaration in Independence Hall. I neatly folded up the Living Economy flag and put it in my bag.

I stood alone in the vast empty lawn of the National Park, looking at Independence Hall in the distance. To gather courage, I repeated to myself: *"Egō nenikēka ton kosmon."* Greek for "I have overcome the world." I took some time to imagine that everything and anything in that building (every person, the police, guns, and my own movements and words) already has the hand of loving destiny behind it. I kept silently repeating those words over and over as I walked to the building, mindfully in rhythm with my footsteps. I focused on the feeling of the soles of my feet on the ground—a practice from when I was a monastic aspirant in Thich Nhat Hanh's tradition, when I was younger. On the way, I glanced at a poster on the wall of a building which said something about an astronomical event called a Venus Transit, which somehow comforted me. For a moment I experienced that I, in this world, was not alone in making a transit.

When I arrived at the gate to the hall grounds, this time I passed smoothly through security, and joined the first tour of the morning.

I wasn't sure how the inside of the building was situated, or what the tour involved. It turned out to be a very brief tour, which ended in the Assembly Hall—the room I was looking for. The room was smaller in real life. The ranger powerfully voiced Thomas Paine's words: "We have it in our power to begin the world over again." Yes. I hastily scribbled those power words onto my paper Declaration. Then he announced: "That's the end the tour folks!"

It was now or never. At that moment, I stepped over the waist-high wooden banister and walked up to John Hancock's desk. I said "don't worry" to the other citizens who were on the tour.[26] I laid my Threefold Declaration right down on the desk where Thomas Jefferson, John Adams, and Benjamin Franklin had signed the other document. I stood there facing Hancock's chair, with my back to the citizenry for a moment, while I signed the paper. It got really quiet.

Then I turned around and held up the Living Economy flag, and extemporaneously voiced the Declaration of Interdependence which Meenal and I had authored. After I finished, the ranger was of course a bit flustered, and said something about "I understand what you all are trying to achieve." And then asked me to leave. I had done what I set out to do, so I draped the flag over my shoulders and walked out the door.

In the foyer, a squad of rangers and police were scrambling. It was chaotic. I just kept steadily walking. People were asking: "Who was it? Where is he?" I was almost to the outside door when one of the rangers said "It's him!" and I was surrounded.

I asked if I was free to go. I was told "No", I was arrested. The police and I recognized each other from talking the previous day. The look on their faces was like: "Well, he made it in after all." One of the more antipathetic men asked heatedly: "What did you break? Did you mark on the desk?" I said: "I didn't break or mark anything. I signed my piece of paper." I was told to drop the flag. I said: "I don't want it to hit the ground."[27] The police said: "We need to see your hands for safety's sake." I said: "I want you to be safe." And I stretched out my arms and hands and held them out so they could see. They relaxed and were then calm and polite, and allowed me to hold the flag to keep it from touching the ground, while we waited to be transported to prison.

---

[26] Afterward I wrote a news article about this action, and a man with a family who had been on the tour wrote to me: "Travis, we were there, part of the tour group. [...] All in all it was a peaceful display of our rights that the founding fathers strived for. Definitely gave us a moment to remember on our tour."

[27] The Threefold America flags are humble enough to touch the earth, yet not in that way.

While we stood there, some police asked about the significance of the patterns and colors. I told them the flag's red square is for Solidarity, the blue stripes are for Fraternity, and the white stripes are the light of Goodwill. The 56 stars are for the economies of the 50 states, the economy of the District of Columbia, and the economies of the 5 U.S. territories. The men liked that I included the territories too. And they said they admired that I'd made it myself.

As I was handcuffed and searched, I asked that the flag be returned to me. The chief officer promised he would. I sensed he was a man of integrity. And he did return it to me the next day.

I experienced two hardships during the arrest and transport—one of the cuffs was accidently clamped on my wrist incorrectly, with the narrow part of the oval painfully jammed across the wide part of my wristbone. I said so, but an officer replied: "We don't recuff." Once I was placed in the police car, there was a long wait, with no officer in sight (as they were in another building dropping my stuff off). The tightness and pain in my wrist, while having my hands behind my back, which compresses the lungs, plus with the windows all the way closed, and AC on (I'm not used to the stale cold air of air-conditioning), resulted in an almost alarming sensation of soul-and-physical suffocation. I focused on breathing steadily and deeply, while silently saying calming words with each breath. In. Out. Deep. Slow. Calm. Ease. Smile. Release.

Through these and other experiences, I have gleaned some tips in regard to interacting with our peace officers in an upright way, which begins to model what a humane future would look like—a future where the police sector is no longer a special class of citizenry. For example, if one is asked for an identification card, then it's simply a matter of spine-straightness to ask for the police officer's identification in return. Yet my story is not about police tactics, so I'm not going to go into all the details.

So. I spent the night in the Federal Detention Center in downtown Philly—a high-rise prison distinguished by its slits for windows.

The FDC in Philly.

There was a prison administrator who was processing the paperwork—his professional nonchalance warmed a bit as I told him about what I did.

As I was being escorted through a corridor, a guard asked about what I'd done...after I told a brief account I said: "You're welcome to join us." He said: "Not me. Because then I'd be in jail."

I was alone in a cell for the day and night. I was only with others when being processed in and out via holding cells. On the way out, I was in a holding cell with a young Mexican man. He had a heavy gang inflection and mannerisms. He spoke of the lurid trauma of the drug war he witnessed in Mexico. I practiced listening deeply, and speaking in a normal way, centered in my heart, and eventually the gangster mannerisms softened, and his accent changed. He told me his story about how many times he's been in jail for immigration or drug violations. He says he feels it is unjust that he is arrested for crossing the border, when California used to be part of Mexico. I replied: "Yes, California is still part of the Mexican cultural homeland." He agreed and was satisfied.

In the Threefold Republic, Mexico would be free to offer its national school system and other voluntary cultural services across political borders, and to show California as a cultural (but not political) territory of Mexico, overlapping with American culture there.

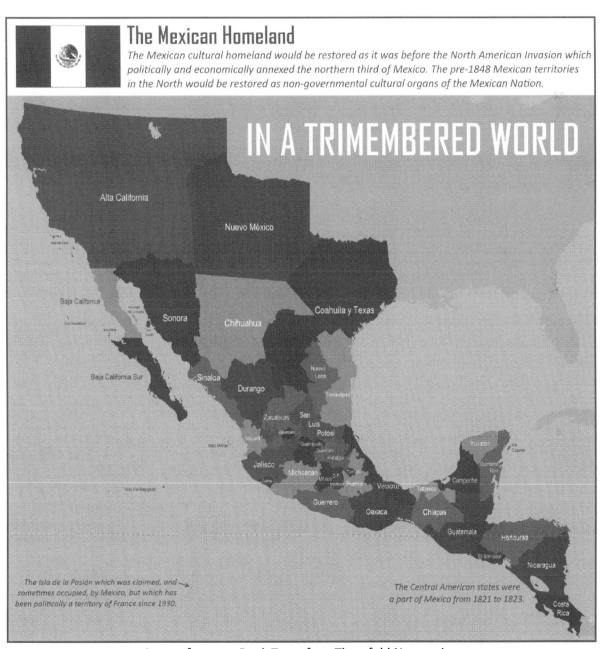

A page from my <u>Book Two</u> of my Threefold Now series.

I was released the next morning. I received a notice with a court date, along with a ban from setting foot in Independence National Park. Actually, I had to return to the park to ask directions to where to pick up my stuff, and the ranger kindly smiled and said: "Well, you're not supposed to be here, but I'll overlook it; here's where you need to go..." My stuff was returned to me in a garbage bag—nothing was missing, except my clothes. As I was sitting on the sidewalk, sorting through my stuff, two Occupiers walked by and asked if I was okay. It turns out one is a local organizer for Philly Occupy, and had heard about my action. He was concerned that such a bold action would frighten the ordinary citizenry and give Occupy a bad name. I realized he didn't know the whole story, so I didn't argue with him. I was just grateful that these two human beings had kindly stopped to console me.

As for my clothes...out of systemic spite, my clothes were to be mailed to my New York address. I walked right back to the front gate of the prison and asked for my clothes. The gatekeeper said no. I said: "Well this is a fitting outfit for America in these times." He smiled and nodded in agreement. So my prison suit became my Occupy/Threefold costume.

That evening, as I was preparing to leave Philadelphia to go home, I was walking through the downtown crowds at night. I needed directions, and as a wave of people were crossing the street, I randomly picked a man to ask directions. The man was strolling casually as if he'd had a leisurely night on the town. As he approached to see what I was asking, he had a quizzical look on his face. Then his face flashed into astonishment—and so did mine—he was the ranger from the tour!

We talked amiably for awhile, and he suggested I might gain something by looking more deeply into Thomas Paine. Then he used his smartphone to look up the directions I needed. Before I left, he asked if he could take a picture of me with my flag. I agreed, then we shook hands and wished each other good luck.

So, that's the main crux of the Philadelphia story.

***

The trek home was an adventure in itself, as I tried to catch up with Occupy's 99-Mile March to from Philadelphia to Wall Street—one of the events I was looking forward to. I myself call it a 100-Mile Parade. The parade left on the day I was released, and so by the time I had gathered my stuff, they were already on their way to New Jersey.

According to the printed schedule, I could still make the first pick-up point, at the train station downtown, so I took the bus there and waited. But the pick-up time passed, with no sign.

Here I was, wearing a prison jumpsuit and carrying my reversed-color flag over my shoulders as a sunscreen. Being "in costume" resulted in a shift into a liminal zone...a doorway to a somewhat different version of myself. People respond differently to one when one is wearing a costume like that. An elderly black man outside the train station said: "He looks like Captain America. Yes, Captain America."

So now what was I going to do? I decided to try to walk the parade route and catch up to them. I figured they would set up camp before dark, so that if I kept walking through the evening, I would reach them. So I set out on foot. It was fitting that I start from the train station, since it's a mile further west from where the march started. That made it a 100-mile march. I was willing to go the extra mile. 99 is not 100.

Long story short, I never found them. I walked about ten miles through North Philadelphia. Let me say, that was a strange place. The "genius loci" had a weird, beautiful, nostalgic feeling at best. A desolate, decaying "zombie apocalypse" vibe at worst. When I first entered that neighborhood, I felt despair and soul distress for awhile. But before long, my second wind kicked in and I felt solid again. It was a lonely walk. I'd never before witnessed city sidewalks which were heaped with mounds of trash with scurrying cockroaches. (In West Virginia, there are some totally trashed rural sites like that, but I'd never in all my travels seen such a desolate urban scene.) Under one yellow street lamp, Klingsorian offerings were openly touted. In another place, there was a derelict, standalone, very dark building with an otherworldly, creepy vibe—I offered a blessing image in thought as I passed by. As the night passed, I laid down to rest in a park which had been kept up beautifully, for which I was grateful, and slept a little, with my Fraternity Flag as a blanket. Then I got up and kept walking till morning. Most everyone would think me foolish for blithely traversing through North Philly at night; but although I wouldn't recommend it to other people, I have had several other rough adventures in life, and no harm has come to me.

When the busses started running again, I took a bus to where I supposed the parade was camped, but I couldn't find them. So in Croydon, a town 20 miles north of Philly, I hitched a ride across the bridge into New Jersey and took a train to Trenton, the next pick-up spot.

On the train, sitting across from me was a beautiful young man with cornrows. He struck up a conversation with me, and was serious and reflective. He asked: "What do you think of my life? I have three girls (partners) in three different cities. What do you think of me?"

In that moment, a feeling of judgment arose instinctively. Then remembering myself, I realized that there is honestly no way I could judge him. All I could authentically do was to wish him the best. I said: "I congratulate you." He nodded and we were silent.

Then I was in the Trenton train station, at the pick-up spot, at the right time...but again no sign of the 99-Mile March.

So I decided this adventure was over. I purchased a train ticket home, and called a friend to pick me up in Wassaic.

When I got home, I shared my experience on the 99-Mile facebook page, and an organizer responded: the team had become overwhelmed with the logistics of the march, and failed to send out the van to the pick-up points, and apologized.

***

Part Two: The Trial

As I was released from the Philadelphia prison, I received a slip of paper with a court date named: "The United States of America versus Travis Henry."

So several weeks later, I drove back down to Philadelphia. From where I live in Upstate New York, it's a 4 hour drive. There were two citations: "Entering a Closed Federal Area" and "Disobeying a Federal Officer."

I took the day off from work. Of course it's an economic strain to miss work—most workers in the American economy do not receive paid personal leave. In this way, one is "economically punished" for challenging the National Law, regardless of whether one is found guilty and actually fined or not.

I could've contacted Occupy Legal Team to ask for help. Yet I felt that my effort was hardly under the Occupy banner. I did though call them like a day or so before the court, just to say that the trial was taking place.

Before I went into the courtroom, I stopped in the bathroom and I put on the prison jumpsuit that I'd received on July 4th.[28] I wasn't there to just be a nice civilian who bows and scrapes, pleading for mercy. I wanted to remind myself, and the court, that it's not a joke.

The defendants who filled the courtroom were almost entirely black males. A young man was fined several hundred dollars for smoking marijuana in the national park. He works as a grocery store clerk—that's several full-days' wages. The judge was a gray-haired older white man, a "liberal" who liked to joke around. Humor can be a good thing, but behind the wisecracking exterior, there was a tired mechanistic routine, and a two-faced sympathy and antipathy. If the defendant said anything in their defense, the judge would get angry, and fine the maximum amount. If one sort of bowed one's head and begged and pleaded, the judge would play the "nice guy" and cut the fine to half (still hundreds of dollars). Either way, no one was found "not guilty"; and the judge would never question the clarity of the prosecutor and police, or the justness of the law itself. The man next to me turned to me and said: "He's going to fine me no matter what—I've got to delay this and get an attorney." Which he did—but that means another day of missed work, plus the cost of hiring an attorney.

Since this is a "petty court", the defendants don't have the right to a public, pro bono attorney. The justification is that these are "minor crimes" and the fines are "only" hundreds of dollars, so it's not worth the State's money to provide a

---

[28] I'm probably one of the few people who own two federal prison jumpsuits...since most prisoners have to turn them in when they are released. But both times I was released with my suit on, so the suits came with me.

defense attorney. But...unlike the lowly individual citizen, the *national government* always has a full-time prosecuting attorney there to speak on *its* behalf, whose job is to prosecute to the maximum extent. The prosecutor and judge see each other day in and day out for years on end. They're friends. They're both employed by the same National Government. Whereas the citizen who passes through is just a nobody, with no connections, who stammers as the two wise-cracking, bantering, well-salaried federal employees work as a tag-team to collect fines. Basically, the courtroom is a revenue collection booth. In actual practice, the separation between the executive branch (police and prosecutor) and judicial branch (the judge) is only theoretical and nominal.

When it was my turn, various rangers were called to testify. Most of their testimony was factual and respectful...I especially appreciated that the honorable ranger (the one who'd kept my flags for me) called my Living Economy flag "an American flag." There was also mention of the $5 I left on John Hancock's desk. Besides the Threefold Declaration, I had left a 5-dollar bill with a note explaining that the money is a tip for the janitor, in thanks for cleaning up the sheet of paper. As a janitor myself, I didn't want to thoughtlessly leave something for someone else to pick up.

But a couple things were distortions or fanciful inventions. For example: one ranger (who wasn't in court, but who only submitted a written testimony) stated that when I was in Independence Hall, I'd said: "Occupy is taking over!"

Which is ridiculous. I hardly even identified with Occupy itself. Maybe the ranger felt like, or feared, that Occupy was "taking over", and then this feeling became mixed in with her memory...but I myself would say no such thing.

In response to that testimony I said: "It's understandable that people misremember things, since it's been several months ago. And I notice that the ranger who wrote that testimony is not actually here to stand by her words. But I said nothing like that. This is what I said." And I turned to the audience and held up the Living Economy flag (I'd brought it with me into the court), and approximately repeated the Declaration of Interdependence I'd voiced at John Hancock's desk.

After that, even the prosecutor stated that she felt the ranger was misremembering!

Which is nice. Perhaps that was one reason why one of the two charges were dropped. But why is such distorted testimony glossed over? If an ordinary citizen was caught distorting the truth, both the prosecutor and judge would pounce on them. At the opening of the court, the judge had made a great show of sternly announcing to the citizenry: "If you tell even the slightest lie, your testimony will be discounted and you will be arrested for contempt of court." Yet then the representative of the National Governance lies. Who will forever discount *its* testimony and hold *it* for contempt of court?

A few excerpts from my testimony: At one point, I said to the judge: "Which of the two party organizations did you swear allegiance to receive your seat here? The one who appointed you...was he a Democrat or Republican?" He only blurted out: "She!"

At another point I was asked if I agree with everything Occupy does. I said: "No, I'm for the best efforts of both the Left and the Right."

...And in a moment of sheer extemporaneity, I told the court that I intend to (peaceably) overthrow the United States, and turn it into a Threefold Republic. I wanted to be able to tell myself after I leave this world, that I went right into the belly of the American beast, and, in its own National Court, spoke words which hardly any American national would even allow themselves to think, much less voice: "I intend to overthrow the United States."

The United States is not God.

In the end, one charge was dropped; for the other I was fined $375. After the sentence was read, I told the judge I would practice refusing to pay the fine. He got angry and assigned me to probation, and commanded the officers to take me to the probation interview room. One of the clerks gasped. It was sorta dramatic.

I told the probation officer in the back room that I would not submit to being under probation (which involves regularly checking in with the probation office, and not travelling a certain distance away from my home). The officer was nice enough. She reminded me of what one of my friends might have been like...if she had not gone to a Waldorf school, and instead of becoming a biodynamic farmer, had gotten a job with the U.S. Government. I declined to answer her questions, saying: "I decline to answer that." The officer said that in all her career, she said she'd never experienced anyone resisting parole. I felt a bit sorry I couldn't have been more personable, but the stress and concern of saying too much or too little—and of having no one to "back me up" and confer with, was too much for me to be nice and chatty. And I didn't know how far I was willing to go that day—I was figuring it out as I went. I preferred not go so far as to be arrested and jailed right then and there, as I had various things to attend to back home. Also, the court had taken so long, that the parking meter on my car was expired—I was worried about that in the back of my mind. Towing fees can be hundreds of dollars. It's these little things that pile up to make for an anti-human experience.

A couple supervisors came in. Out of the many questions they asked me, one turned out to be a trick. He asked: "Are you a sovereign citizen?" I didn't know what he was talking about, but I liked the sound of "sovereign citizen." Those are beautiful words. Who would deny being a sovereign citizen? So I said: "Yes I am." That's one of the few questions I answered, along with a list of the countries I've visited (I don't care if the U.S. knows I've travelled humanity's world). In retrospect, the "sovereign citizen" tidbit is probably one thing which led to me being approached with a heavily armed force. I found out later that the "Sovereign Citizens" are a specific movement of individuals who are trying to supersede the U.S. national law; and there have been some armed run-ins, so that the words "Sovereign Citizen" has been marked as a kind of "domestic terrorist." Who knew? It evokes a picture of a future where our police have their own internal law which is not generally known to the ordinary citizenry, and which would require a citizen to have a high-paid lawyer on hand at all times to navigate even the simplest police interaction without being sucked into the Black Hole.[29]

Eventually we were done and I left.

Part Three: One Jail and Two Prisons

When I returned home, I immediately wrote a "Letter on the Nation's Probation", and sent it to the Federal Probation Office, saying that if the National Government wishes to speak with me again, it's welcome to send a representative to come and talk with me.

The house in upstate New York where I was living at the time.

---

[29] Something my dad said once comforts me though: he said that even Black Holes make music—they tone they sing is B Flat.

The FBI (U.S. national police) called and interviewed me. The officer was an American Indian from the Mohawk Nation. He said he respected my efforts to make national amends to the American Indians and Blacks. He said that several witnesses stated that I intend to overthrow the United States.[30] He offered that I meant to overthrow the United States through non-violent means, such as voting. I affirmed that my effort to replace the United States with a Threefold Republic is non-violent. But he said he was not sure how the Probation Office would respond.

When I told a friend the FBI had called, the friend spontaneously and poignantly offered to stand in the way of them. Oh dear!

One morning, a few weeks later, a ten-man, armored SWAT team of Federal Marshals came in the front door of our house. They had commandeered a housemate to lead them to my room, and they then banged my bedroom door as if I was a military target. My noble friend had the presence of mind to vocably warn: "They have guns!" I arose to an assault rifle aimed at my chest. I smiled and went with them.

I was transported to a court hearing in Albany, the capital of New York State. On the way, the marshals (who are mostly ex-soldiers and marines), talked almost entirely about sports. Except that two of them had grown up on dairy farms, and one was arguing the benefits of pesticides and synthetic hormones, while the other was for organic farming. He ended the argument by saying: "Conventional milk is just milk-flavored pesticides."

Along the way, the men kindly loosened up my leg-chains to make the ride more comfortable.

Eventually, all of the marshals were dropped off, except for one, who was to drive me to the court. He asked me: "You are someone who knows what you're talking about. Do you support Democrats or Republicans?" I said: "I support neither. I'm for the Threefold Republic." He asked if there's something he could read about that, and I directed him to my website, and he thanked me.

Entering the courtroom, one of the bailiffs laughed to see me in pajamas and chains. I turned and said: "I'm proud to be in my pajamas. It's a fitting outfit for America in these times. I'd rather be standing here in my pajamas than wearing that uniform and standing where you are." He sobered up.

A pro bono lawyer was assigned to me, but I dismissed him, because I felt that the entire legal profession is entangled with systemic illness. I mean, he's employed by the same entity that was holding me in prison.

There was an array of federal representatives—the judge and various clerks—all sitting on an elevated, u-shaped dias in front of me. The female staff were all dressed up in the chic office raiment that a federally-salaried worker can afford. I refused to sit, so that, by standing, I would be eye-to-eye with them.

The prosecuting attorney started out with: "Travis Henry was born in Princeton, West Virginia, lives in Columbia County, New York, and has been to China, Canada, Mexico, Germany, Austria, Hungary, Romania, Moldova, Pridnestrovie, and Ukraine. We request that his passport be surrendered."

The judge kept asking robotic questions as to whether I am really "Travis Henry." I replied: "I mean no disrespect to you, or to any other individual in this room, but these questions are idiotic. The United States is a half wit. Obviously, I am Travis Henry."

He asked if I cared whether I would be released or not. I said: "As a human being, I would rather go home. Why not just unlock these cuffs and let me go?"

There was a moment of shifting silence.

---

[30] The U.S. law on sedition states that only *violent* overthrow ("overthrow by force") is unlawful. Freely speaking of non-violent overthrow is a legal right.

The judge asked if I would return for the next court date. I said: "No, I would go about my daily business."

The judge commanded the marshals to hold me until the trial. At least I kept my passport. :)

I sensed it was refreshing for the marshals to hear I was hard on the judge. The marshal re-cuffed me solemnly. On the way out, the bailiff who had chuckled nodded seriously and I nodded back. The marshals dropped me in the county jail.

The Rensselaer County Jail in Troy, near Albany.

The county jailers said they didn't know what to do with me, as they had no record of why I was there. They said all the marshals said was: "hold him."

At first I simply was not going to cooperate with filling out paperwork or anything else—and I politely yet firmly said so. It was fine by me to stay "unprocessed" in the holding cell. Seeing me in my pajamas, the first guard—a younger fellow—thought I was a crazy person who was picked up off the street, and so our interactions were shaky.

In the holding cell, I heard one of my friends call on the phone. I could hear his voice over the speaker phone at the guard station across the room. That was a comfort.

The guard eventually called for the opinion of another guard, who called for the shift manager, and when I explained what happened, he understood and spoke with me sensibly.

One guard looked up my website on the internet, and read part of my Letter aloud:

> "I will help you understand. *You*, the United States, are the one who is on probation; *you* are being probed and tried by Humanity and the Times:
>
> *"Over the bleached bones and jumbled residues of numerous civilizations are written the pathetic words: "Too late."*
>
> —Martin Luther King, Jr., *The World House*

Then I was brought to a proper cell, where I was in solitary quarantine for some days. There is a medical quarantine time for all arriving inmates; yet my time was delayed, because I refused a tuberculosis prick. The guards said that I wouldn't receive mail until I took the TB test. In retrospect, it is a prisoner's right to receive mail, regardless of whether they are in quarantine or not.

I spent much of the time singing, along with imagining what a full-blown Threefold evolutionary movement would require. (For example, I worked out the details of how existing secessionist groups would be brought into a Threefold Movement. From a systemic perspective, the Threefold Republic is the only idea which will unify such diverse and seemingly adversarial groups.)

Some of the sheriff deputies came to my cell to talk with me, and agreed with some of the things I'm aiming for. One man thought I was for New York State or the local Counties seceding from the United States. He said: "We're not for the Feds. We're for the County." I said "That will be true on the day when Rensselaer County supersedes the United States." Those words evoked a kind of thrill or spark in the men. But I explained that I'm only for secession as a means to become a Threefold Republic.[31] The world doesn't need another nation-state. As the deputies were leaving, one said: "You're not alone."

Eventually, I decided that my body is strong enough to shrug off any TB injection. I just wanted to get on with it. I agreed to speak with a senior officer, and was escorted to an office. I said: "I am a human being, so of course I wish to have contact with my loved ones."

After taking the TB prick, then I received my barcoded wristband. The officer (a Christian woman) said earnestly to me: "this isn't the Beast, it's just a barcode."

***

When I was finally released into the dayroom, it was sensory overload. After days in silent, solitary twilight, going into a shared, din-thronged, echoing space, with two televisions blaring, was stunning. Luckily, I could go back to my room and close the door whenever I wished. That evening, I received my first visit from friends.

Over the course of those couple weeks, several friends came and visited me in jail during the visiting hour. At first, they didn't know what had happened, and feared something unsavory and very dark. Some people in the town where I live, such as the post-office clerks, were seriously considering how to protest my disappearance.

It was so good to see my friends. One thing I especially remember was how one friend taught me a meditation, which I did each day while I was in jail.

I was sorry to hear that even going through the visitor process—the long wait to be allowed into the visitor room, and interacting with a gruff and ill-willed guard—was at times harrowing in itself.

Then there was mail. To receive a letter was a treasure. I felt rich to be held in the souls of others.

One of the hardest things was that I didn't have any access to a pen and paper. When I was in quarantine for several days, I kept asking for something to write with. The jailers said that pens had to be purchased through the commissary, and that I wouldn't have commissary until I was released from quarantine. I discovered that even after I was released into the dayroom, ordering through the commissary would take a week for a pen to arrive. I did borrow a pen from another prisoner, but had to return it after I was done. I was feeling frustrated about not having a writing utensil, because I needed to write down what fresh ideas were coming to me, and to make notes about the arrest and trial, and to respond to the precious mail I was receiving from friends.

This is how I finally got a pen: in the prisoner rulebook that was handed to me upon arrival, I noticed that the "right to mail service" is a fundamental right of inmates in New York State. Then I noticed that on the "prisoner communications computer" there was a way to file a formal complaint. So I filed a complaint, saying that my right to correspond through mail was effectively hindered by tying it to the commissary. If it was a *right*, then, like soap, I had a *right* to access the basic means to write letters, regardless of whether I had any money in the commissary or not. So I was called to speak with the

---

[31] In fact, the original purpose for which I had made the Threefold America flags was to begin an effort to form a Threefold Republic in Columbia County, N.Y. I had received a micro-grant from Credere, a local Threefolding foundation, to that end.

captain of the entire jail. In his office, he agreed with me, and gave me a little pen. Jail pens are not like normal pens; they are tiny, soft, and bendy. And he gave me some sheets of paper. Whew!

The captain is a servant of Equality. I acknowledged that.

Get this though: on the walk back to my cell, I dropped the tiny pen and lost it!!! Oh woe is me!!! The agony of defeat.

...But I told my tragic story to the guard on duty, and she kindly went into a cell that was being cleaned out, and found not one, but *two pens*, and gave them to me! I felt rich and my heart swelled with gratitude.

I wrote a public letterwhile I was in the county jail—it's inspired by Thoreau. My friends uploaded it to my website:

Wow. I guess the United States needs that $375 badly if It sends a helmeted SWAT team of amply-salaried Federal marshals to my bedroom, with guns drawn and a trigger-ready assault rifle aimed at my chest.
Bless those mens' hearts.

I see that the United States is half-witted, that It is timid as an old man with his silver spoons, and that It does not know Its friend from Its foes. I lose all my remaining respect for It, and pity It.

Yet my cordial adversary—in Its own words, this adventure is called "The United States versus Travis Henry"—has enough funds to pay the County jail to forcibly hold my body at the cost of $110 a day. At ten days so far, and no definitive end in sight, perhaps the United States really has enough money after all.
This affirms for me that the Governance of the American People is not an organization I desire to support in any way.

I question Humanity in America, lest the moment of time for the comprehension of the Threefold Idea and the enactment of the Threefold Republic slip by and be lost:

- ▼ *Who will issue an arrest warrant to the United States and guarantee to stop Its wicked corporatist militarism?*
- ▼ *Does the United States think It's too big to jail?*
- ▼ *Is there any god, concept, idea, or human being which might stand taller than the Power of the United States?*
- ▼ *Whose dominion will penetrate and prevail regardless of cost?*
- ▼ *What would a completed United States look like, with Its heart turned from metal into flesh?*

In liberty, equality and fraternity,
Travis Henry
Prisoner # 1035375

A circle of friends stepped in to fill various roles. One friend went and talked with the managers at the grocery store where I work, and let them know that I would be gone for awhile. Another friend did legal research; she called around to keep tabs on the case. (From within the prison, one hardly knows what's going on, even with one's own case.) With another I shared my bank info with so he could transfer some of my money for use in the commissary. Another mailed me sheet music for songs to sing. Another served as the go-to person for communications, to receive emails and enquiries from friends and acquaintances.

Recently a friend asked if there was any media coverage of my story. I believe there was a local reporter who was contacted by my friends at the time, but I think they got the sense that the reporter would not be empathetic, and might portray me as a "crazy person." So it wasn't pursued. I don't yet know of any journalist, whether they be conservative or liberal, who would not think I'm crazy for trying to separate business, state, and education.

The County Jail. Though not visible here, a black flag flies over the jail...
...the POW/MIA flag, which I call the "Endless War Flag."

Other anecdotes from the jail in Troy:

The chair incident. So, I sat down in an empty chair. There are not an abundance of chairs. A few minutes later, a young man came up and said: "That's my chair." I said: "I don't see any names on the chairs." He left in a huff. Then a couple friends came back with him and made their case. His friend said: "Look, how would you feel if you had been sitting in the same chair for weeks and months, and then one day, someone takes it. It's a matter of fairness and rights." I was astonished that he called upon the sense of rightness, and though I wasn't entirely in agreement with the reasoning, I admired that he had appealed to what was fair. So, I gracefully shifted to another chair at the table. Over time, I witnessed that it's true that many of the men do choose to sit in the same chair, and that this was his customary chair. Fine.

One thing I did was to join in, or watch men play, the boardgame Risk. These guys were really into it, with marathon sessions lasting several hours.

I only sat in front of the television screen for two showings, to see *The Wizard of Oz* and *Star Wars Episode One: The Phantom Menace*. I look forward to the Winkies eventually joining Dorothy in pouring water on the Wicked Witch of the West. And I felt like Obi-Wan Kenobi in the pit, hanging by his hands, his lightsaber gone, and with Darth Maul growling and glaring down at me.

As for reading: a friend gifted me with a copy of MLK's *Why We Can't Wait*, which I read for the first time. I include his "Ten Commandments for the Nonviolent Movement" in Book Two of my Threefold Now series.

In one conversation with a meth dealer named "Scratch" (or was it "Itch"?), he said: "If ordinary jobs had been plentiful, so I could provide for my family, I wouldn't have become a drug dealer."

The architecture of the jail is very similar to the architecture of the government (public) school I attended as a youth, with the usual "Institutional American" style: painted cinderblock with plastic-rubber baseboard trim. It's almost as if both were extensions of an "aesthetic world" into which much or most of American humanity is conditioned to feel at home within.

44

As far as prison food goes: I've been mostly vegetarian for about 15 years. Food in the jail and prisons was basically like government (public) school cafeteria food. For the first couple days, I felt soul distress about the institutional, chemically food. I even talked with a guard about the possibility of vegetarian fare, but what that meant was more canned vegetables and peanut butter sandwiches. And I've found in the past the hydrogenated pb feels more harmful to my body than meat, so I soon decided I was just going to enjoy reverting to my teenage-era American tastes, and eat what appealed to me from what was offered, even if it be chicken sandwiches and hamburgers. Ugh! It tasted okay though. And I would detox once I got out. If I had been sentenced to months, then I might have pursued the veggie option. There have been other times in my biography when I've been in a rough spot, and have serenely practiced "eating what is set before me." Goodness knows it's not my preference.

I was in Troy for Thanksgiving, and enjoyed the turkey and pumpkin pie. I thought of my friends warmly feasting together in Harlemville.

I took advantage of the daily exercise times, when those who wished to were led to the gym. Only a few would choose to go (didn't want to miss any television?). Near the roof was a large barred opening through which fresh air and skylight flowed in. I would walk the perimeter and sing to myself. The Mexicans would come to the gym just to sing. One of the guards liked their singing and would make requests for English-language songs. I requested a Spanish song, which they gave, and in exchange, I sang "Firmly on the Earth I Stand", for which they thanked me.

One phenomenon to look out for: is when a low-minded person tries to insinuate that one is "crazy" if one does something different. Instead of watch television all day, I would often walk the perimeter of the pod. Walking kept me physically active and helped me think freshly. But one inmate—who looked exceedingly acclimated to jail life—kind of rolled his eyes and made a "loco" symbol towards me just because I would rather walk than vegetate. It's not like it was a little room...where I'd understand that walking could be distracting...the pod is a large place. I had experienced this kind of challenge before in my travels: such persons are actually expressing their fear of the craziness they grew up with. I shrugged it off and ignored him.

The pod where I was stationed was not high-security. There was one guard for the whole pod, who sat in boredom at a console in the midst of the dayroom. Sometimes the guard was female. It was not such an intense place—just a county jail.

Some guard interactions:

One of the guards had been a policeman in Philmont, the village where I lived. We talked about Philmont, and he asked what the national anthem would be in a Threefold Republic.[32]

As I was being escorted to and from my cell one day, a guard sincerely expressed to me that his feelings were hurt by reading the words from Thoreau which he read on my "What Is Teotl?" webpage:

"Visit the Navy Yard, and behold a marine, such a man as an American government can make, or such as it can make a man with its black arts—a mere shadow and reminiscence of humanity [...] The mass of men serve the state thus, not as men mainly, but as machines, with their bodies."

—Thoreau, *Resistance to Civil Government*

He said: "I'm not just a machine." He said it with a tone of human hurt.

Another time, a gatekeeper asked: "What do you think of this jail?"

---

[32] I didn't have an answer for him, because I wasn't feeling eloquent enough in the moment to explain how the national-cultural identities would be separated from the Rights Republic. The "national cultures" would keep their traditional anthems, such as the "Star-Spangled Banner" for the US national culture. However, what I would suggest for a "rights anthem" is the song "We Each Live in the Other" from the poet Novalis, which has been put to music by a music teacher I know from Philmont.

I said : "This is best jail I've ever visited." Which is true: the Surry County, North Carolina jail and the Bernalillo County, New Mexico jail I was in during my younger hobo days were not as nice.

He smiled and nodded.

Another photo of the County Jail.

I had not decided how far I would take this. The longer option was to be sentenced to 6 months in prison. And if I resolved to never pay tribute to the United States again, I suppose I would be in prison forever.

Yet my heart melted when one friend's eyes watered and told me to come home. So I affirmed that the priority now was to extract myself from the gears of this machine, so that I could write the books which could form the conceptual basis for a Threefold Republic. Since then, I've written four books, and have several more on the way. Every book that I finish, is another public resource that will be there if and when the time comes for me to engage with the U.S. nation-state again.

As I was leaving the Troy jail, I was in a holding cell with a young Mohawk man who was there for dealing marijuana. Based on the quantity, he probably will be there a long time. I felt sorrow about how even the Haudeonsaunee (Iroquois) way of life is not vigorous and pervasive enough.

On the way out, I said to the guards that I look forward to the day when we put a new flag patch on their uniform. One of the guards seemed distressed at the prospect, and I felt sorry for stirring his waters. The other guard smiled and said: "Great!" (I like his attitude.)

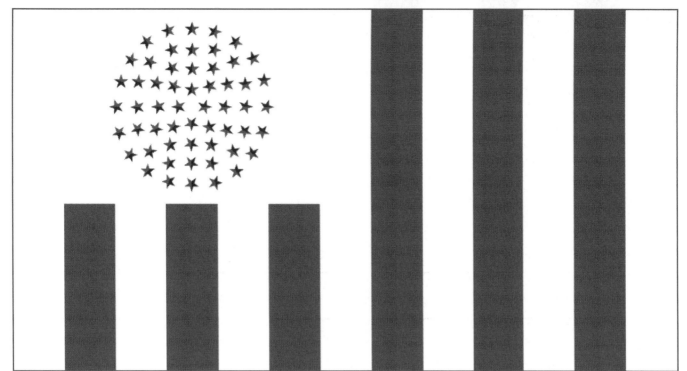

A flag patch for an egalitarian Rights Governance purified of all party organizations, wealth-based laws, and corporate-purchased rights. Where each adult citizen has an equal voice, and where economic and cultural lobbies have no voice whatsoever. Colorwise, each star and stripe is half-blue, half-red.

***

Next I was driven in a van to a Federal Prison in New York City.

As we were pulling in, the especially sour, stern face on all of the guards was clearly evident. One man next to me asked: "Why do their faces look like that?" I said, "It's the Federal Spirit in them." Some other men were like: "What is he talking about?" But the man said: "Listen. I think he's onto something."

What I mean is that there is a certain esprit-de-corps in any organization, and this was visible on their faces.

I signed in with a triangle and 3 as my signature. The guard said: "What's this?" I said that's my symbol—I'm a political prisoner. He asked: "What kind of political prisoner?" I said "I'm with Occupy." His eyes lit up, and the sour, deadened "federal mask" fell for a moment.

One phenomenon to look out for: in prison there is occasionally a type of person who expresses their human fear by exaggerating how terrible something is going to be. Like, as we were approaching the strip search station, one young man was like: "Yo, that guard is going to tear us apart! He's a bull!" It's best to ignore such persons as they are temporarily demented.

The Metropolitan Detention Center in Brooklyn.
The big square windows on the near side, are the exercise yards of each pod.

I was supposed to have another TB prick! I was incredulous...I said it was unhealthy to have two TB exposures in so close in time. The Feds wouldn't accept a TB prick taken by a County jail...only a Federal TB prick. I said: "Look, your Federal court put me in a County jail. The County jail was good enough to serve as your subcontractor. If the County was good enough to hold a Federal prisoner, then the County TB shot is good enough too." I wrote a one page explanation about that and my spiritual distaste for unnecessary vaccinations (as far as I know, the prick gives a little dose of TB). The nurse rolled her eyes at the length, saying "A whole page?" (There are some dense situations where I'm vulnerable to people thinking I'm a "crazy brainy guy.") I requested that the letter be placed in my file. Then I just took the prick. Again, I just wanted to get on with it, and trusted my body is strong enough to shake it off. The actual test was administered by another nurse, who as she pricked me, I said to her: "I bless you, because you are cursing me." She kindly said: "I'm not cursing you." I said: "You aren't cursing me, but the U.S. System is cursing me through you."

Anyway, vaccination is not my main battle, so, beyond making symbolic effort, I didn't worry about it.

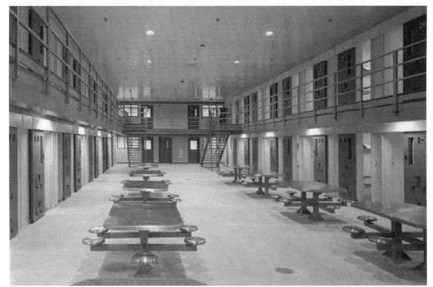
The MDC insides are all metal, like a navy battleship.

There, I made friends with two young men from Ghana and Benin who were interested in what a Threefold Republic would look like in Africa. My Ghanaian friend said: "I want you to not be taken by the U.S. government again, because it is necessary for you, as a leader, to not be squelched before the movement can unfold." He asked me to send him a book of Threefold Africa pictures when I got out. He gave me his address, and approved that I'd written it in faint, tiny letters on an inconspicuous piece of paper, which I kept with me through the rest of my prison journey. He was interested in the stories of humanosophic Christology which I told when were in a holding cell together. When I was released, I did make a booklet for him and mailed it to his mother to give to him someday. I haven't heard from him yet.

Of course, there were lots of meaningful interactions like that with inmates and guards—but for brevity's sake, I'm only touching on a few highlights.

For example, there was an elderly Ojibwe man in there. I greeted him with: "Elder, would you tell me a story?" He told me about his grandson, saying: "Even though he has brown eyes, his eyes sometimes have sparks of golden light. At first I didn't believe it, but I see we can have colored eyes too."[33]

In my renewed quest to have access to an envelope and stamp, I was called to speak with a clerk in the administrative area outside of the pod. She was helpful—and gave me the pointer to always remember the full name of any administrator I speak with. She did speak up for me to get a stamp; her supervisor said to me that if I dropped a letter into the mailbox, he would put a stamp on it. In retrospect, that letter never arrived. I don't know what the supervisor did with the letter, but I witnessed that the clerk did try to help me.

I talked a lot with a Romanian fellow who looked and talked very much like Robert Di Nero. He was passionately interested in ancient Dacian culture, and I was one person who had something to say about that. So we talked about the various theories for how ancient Dacians turned into modern-day Romanians.

I made one clear mistake. I needed a shower kit, but there was no guard there at the office. Receiving a shower kit is a daily routine. I waited, but no guard. The kits were hanging there, almost in reach. So I stepped into the doorway and picked a kit off the rack—but a guard saw me from a distance, from across the pod. He came up and said: "What are you doing in my space?!" I knew I'd gone too far, so was apologetic, and pointed to the shower kit. He grumbled, and I went on my way.

Later though, after I'd rested, I realized that I was not only slightly mistaken...it was actually wrong to enter the guard's space. It was a transgression of their legitimate human need for defined space. Soulwise, these men and women are

---

[33] This was especially meaningful to me because I'd been recently thinking about that myself. I had met an Asian Indian friend whose black/brown eyes had golden sparks of light, and I was wondering about that.

surrounded, day in and day out, by prisoners of all stripes, and need to feel secure. These people need to have at least one bounded space. I realized I had an amends to make. So when I saw the guard again (he's a Jamaican man), I simply apologized: "I was wrong to enter into your space. That was disrespectful, and I apologize." He nodded.

Brooklyn was the first time I had a cellmate. I had two different cell-mates there. One a white drug dealer. The other a black churchman, also there for drug issues, and who was carrying some weight. With the first, our conversation was poignantly centered on how much sorrow would have been side-stepped if the War on Drugs had never happened. With the other fellow, I shared about the difficulties I've had with food, and how I've approached physical, emotional, and spiritual recovery. He said he'd been thinking about just this very thing, and he voiced an aspiration to cut out white sugar and white flour. I know from hard experience how recovery is often a zig-zag path, but that's what we talked about.

At the Brooklyn prison, the exercise yards are directly attached to each pod, and are available at any time during the day. I would often go out there to walk around, breathe fresh air, kick the soccer ball, and to sing.

***

Then, I was bussed to the Philadelphia prison where I'd spent the night back on July 4th. This was a prison bus, with everyone shackled hand and foot.

I had a cellmate in Philadelphia. A white man there for alleged gun possession. We mostly minded our own business. Hearing of his own rage about how the guards reportedly dickered with access to communication with his wife, was a stark reminder of the need to stay serene; and how inordinate dislike from one or more guards or prison officials could result in subtle or blatant hindrances.

As I was being escorted to a holding cell, the guard asked: "Are you a Sovereign?"
This indicates that the answer I'd given back in July as to whether I'm a "sovereign citizen," was apparently noted in the record and disseminated.
I replied: "I'm a Threefolder."
He asked: "What's that?"
I said: "I'm for the separation of business, state, and education."

In the holding cells, it was interesting to see the dynamic between the street dealer (a powerfully charismatic Black fellow) and the Italian mafia. The mafiosos were there for court, and filed by in expensive suits, with a lawyer in front of them. The streetman was in the cell. The streetman and the mafia greeted each other by name, with the eerily cordial tone of hardened humanity.

Also, to see the gang spirit as a formative force. In humanosophic language, I would name these as Luciferian petty archangeloi. They are impressive, and reformulate the speech and mannerisms of the human individual who is initiated and filled with that group persona. Gang spirits arise where the landscape has been turned into a Mephistophelean "bone-scape" of concrete. The gang archangeloi fill and enliven these empty, desolate cityscapes. They also arise where the Mephistophelean pressure is so great, such as in prison. The counterparts of gang spirits are the spirits of police departments (gangbusters) and the spirits of prison facilities, which are Mephistophelean archangeloi. (In everyday language, Luciferian is "harm done by rebels"; Mephistophelean is the "harm done by authorities.")

I was in a holding cell with Latin Kings (a.k.a. "The Almighty Latin King and Queen Nation"). The familial warmth displayed to each other and the code-switching from English to Spanish and Spanish to English in the middle of their sentences, was not unbeautiful.

Lastly, there was a court appearance. Because now I had decided to go through the motions necessary to extract myself, I accepted the court-appointed attorney—a young New Yorker whose demeanor reminded me of one of my friends. He was warm about Occupy, and I didn't mind working with him to get this over with.

There was court clerk who was sitting up on the dias waiting for the judge to arrive, and for my hearing to begin. As I was telling my story to my lawyer, the clerk couldn't hear what we were talking about; but when I got to the place in the story where the SWAT team approached my door, my hands unthinkingly made a gesture of how the men came to me with the gun toward my chest. The clerk worriedly exclaimed: "It looks like you're pointing a gun!" Anyway, the lawyer smiled and shrugged it off—he knew I was just telling the story. But I felt sorrow about that gesture—I don't want anyone to feel afraid.

In the meantime, some of my friends had gathered the $375 and paid the court. (I paid my friends back later. It was never about the money. I paid tribute to my friends, and my friends paid tribute to my effort.) The prosecutor requested that I be released from prison and from probation. The prosecutor was the same who had prosecuted me in the original trial. She could've dickered with me, but to her credit, she didn't.

As I was leaving the courtroom, a Probation Officer approached me to fill out paperwork which would close out the parole. One of the questions was: "Do any females or children live in your house? If so, how many? What are their names?" Of course the "ordinary" reason for this question is to protect the innocent civilians should the State decide their house needs to be invaded. The deeper reason is to insinuate into the parolee's mind that one's loved ones are hostages of the Military-Corporatist State. The look in my eye expressed this: "If you think I'm going to name the names of my loved ones, you can just f***ing put me back in the prison." He said: "Well, let's just skip that one."

Before I was released, a marshal checked my pockets, and in the process, spilled some small coins. In the practiced nonchalance typical of soldiers, he was going to leave the coins, as a subtly demeaning gesture. I said: "Why don't you pick those up. That's my property. If I had littered like that, you would have me pick it up." He picked them up and pointed to the President's face on the coin, saying: "See that face, that's the face of the U.S. Government. If you're trying to make a new society, why do you have this coin in your pocket?"

I said: "In the Threefold Republic, the currency will be issued by the Economic Associations, not by the Government."

He smiled brightly, and handed the coins back to me.

Another of the marshals, a black man, was from Hinton, West Virginia, near where I grew up. We reminisced about the beautiful park beneath Bluestone Dam, where my brothers and I used to play when we were kids.

In a holding cell on the way out, one young man leaped and yelled at me, thinking he'd startle me. I just laughed. I'd experienced that "let's try to startle a passerby" trick before during my "Okie" time in urban California. I suppose some inexperienced persons mistakenly take my spectacled appearance, and think I'm only mild. I felt no disturbance, and he went on his way.

The last man in my holding cell wore a kufi and beard. He said to me: "In the state prison, you have to be a member of a gang to survive. Since you're white, you'd be with the Nazis."

I nonchalantly replied: "Not going to happen. I would be myself."

After that, we relaxed and talked about various things. I asked him: "You're a Muslim?"
He replied: "I'm an educated Muslim."
I said: "I'm a friend of Allah."
He said: "No you're not. Anyone who is not a friend of Allah will be burned on judgment day."
I responded with "Bless you." We were silent the rest of the time.

Until the end, when he asked: "May I have your subway token? The guards will give you a subway token when you leave."

I said: "If I had a subway token, I would give it to you. Because I don't need it."

He smiled.

He was released before me, and I never received a subway token anyway.

***

I was released onto the street on a winter night, with a jumpsuit, t-shirt, and slippers. I believe the date was December 6th, 2012. I felt like Luke Skywalker falling out of the bottom of Cloud City. I considered what it would take for me to make it back home using only my own resources. I have made some rough journeys; yet not in the middle of winter, in the Northeast, with zero money, without adequate clothing. Even for my most "adventurous self", that was not an option. My eyes dimmed.

I bummed a quarter and called my friends. Luckily, one of my friends had a friend who lives in Philly. I waited for her under the statue of the Lenape Chief Tammany down by the riverfront. I had visited that statue during the Occupy parade back in July.

I put my arms inside my jumpsuit and walked vigorously back and forth in front of the statue, singing to keep warm. The friend appeared and took me to her house and gave me some of her brother's spare clothes, got some food in me, and took me to the train station.

Arriving back home in Philmont, I was supposed to call the Albany Probation Office to finalize the release from probation. When I called, the man said "You were supposed to check in on the same day you were released." Obviously, since I was released in the evening, into a strange city, and didn't get home till 3 am in the morning, it was not feasible. He agreed that it was not realistic to have checked in that same day. He then affirmed that I was no longer under probation.

A few weeks later, a friend and I returned to Troy to pick up my stuff, such as letters which friends had written. The guard at the entrance (a soulful-eyed person) checked on my stuff, but we had missed the cut-off date, and the stuff was tossed. Oh well. It was a good closure just to see the place from the outside, with a friend at my side.

***

Part Four: The Aftermath

All total, it was an 18-day adventure.

Before this, I had been in jail a couple times before, from my footloose days when I was younger, and have been on various other "rough" adventures in North America and abroad. So the experience of police and jails was not new or terrible.

Afterward, a friend asked if I was ever afraid. One tense spot was when I was in a large group of prisoners who were being processed out of the Brooklyn MDC, with our hands and feet chained—and the federal guards were yelling at me for some reason (I think it was because I asked about whether my few belongings would be shipped with me or not), and when I tried to explain, he would interrupt me. He yelled: "I don't even want to hear one word from you! Not even a breath!" I didn't know what to do, so I started singing "Firmly on the Earth I Stand, Michaël's Sword Within My Hand." The guards got quiet and the cell full of prisoners too. I sang the verses, and when I finished, the situation was different. My Romanian friend smiled and said: "You are truly a revolutionary."

But the two most difficult experiences were not in the prison. The most emotionally challenging aspects were:

1) Knowing what to say in the courtrooms—to speak in an upright way, congruent with my values, without just going along with the thick cloud of convention that surrounds the proceedings. I practiced the directions from the Gospel of Luke: *"But whenever they bring you to assemblies before rulers and authorities, you shall not be concerned how you will give an answer or what you will say."* But still I would feel remorse afterward about saying too much or too little, too meekly or too stridently.

And 2), the very most difficult part of the whole experience was witnessing the strain in my friends...and meeting that with my own strain...as this experience extended beyond the everyday boundaries of our souls.

***

Here are some post-prison responses (both challenging and affirming) which I experienced:

On the week of my return, my closest circle of friends and I met, and we basically ended up in an ugly argument. In retrospect, it would've been better to have a "wise elder" facilitating the meeting. I myself was hardly there...my everyday self had not fully returned yet. May I remember to give any friend who comes home from prison at least a week of downtime before engaging in any hard back-and-forth.

I experienced a bit of concern from the local Anthroposophic community that the eye of the local public, and the eye of the U.S. government, might turn toward and against them. This was (understandably) heightened by their not knowing then how far I was going to go, and whether my actions or words would result in the dilemma of them having to choose whether to openly associate with me, or to disclaim me as a wildcard. I understand that this coolness was also a legitimately well-intentioned gesture—to not contribute toward "inciting" and "riling" me.

Another challenge: housemates were, understandably, a bit traumatized by the police invasion. I was and am remorseful for not giving my housemates a warning ahead of time. I did tell one housemate, but I wasn't experienced enough yet to know whether the usual response for resisting a petty misdemeanor would be anything more than a letter.

Some times in the following months, I wondered if there was a subtle unease around me, as if I were a "marked man." For example, one friend who was visiting the U.S. was briefly concerned that associating with me (as a person with a criminal record) might somehow result in a mark in their records and make it difficult for them to cross the border. That's understandable, but they quickly brushed it aside. Anyway, probation was cancelled as soon as the fine was paid, at the same time I was released from prison. Yet even a couple years later, an acquaintance asked me in passing: "Are you cleared of all the charges and probation yet?" The fact that that was something on their mind (out of all the things one could ask about my effort) shows that there is a fear in the back of the mind of being "marked" by the National Authorities. To that I would say: the Good authorities can make marks too.

I was incredulous that one Anthroposophic friend implied that I was naively influenced by rascally Occupiers! Something like: "If it weren't for those radical Occupiers, Travis would've just been a nice Anthroposophist." No. If you knew me well, you would know that I clearly saw both the beauty and the one-sidedness of Occupy before stepping into the National Gathering. I don't especially favor the Left (or the Right). I acted under my own banner, though within the context of Occupy. I went in with my own individual impulse, and never significantly strayed from that.

Another friend wondered whether I had "provoked" the police into coming they way they did, with SWAT gear and so forth. Yet I wrote the "Letter on the Nation's Probation" with only two focuses: a full heart and an upright spine. I literally invited the representatives of the United States to come and talk with me. I was simply done with driving for hours to go to some robotic court. Outside of that letter, there are other points in the story where I did say some words which were sharper than what most people are used to ("I aim to (peaceably) overthrow the United States"). In these times, forthrightness can be misperceived as provocation. But yes, perhaps my words could be called *pro-voking*, in the literal sense that I did "call forth" some events to unfold. I certainly didn't try to "avoid punishment", because that simply wasn't my goal.

Another (who was otherwise supportive) said something unsavory: "prison is a dangerous place for a 'nice white guy.' And the system can eat you up." (!) Disregarding the implication that prison *isn't a dangerous place for other colors of guys*...since my friend is in close friendship with Black Humanity, so I know she didn't mean it that way...the words still rub me the wrong way. For one thing, I'm not such a "nice" guy. And, another thing: I'm not so "white." Besides having Powhatan Indian ancestors, I grew up in West Virginia, the second poorest state in the country, in a notoriously rough coal-mining community. In my twenties, I lived for four years in a neighborhood in south Greensboro where I was, as far as I know, the only Caucasian. When I went to vote, I was the only "white" person in a gymnasium full of people. I haven't lived a "nice" life...for much of my life I've worked at gas stations. And when I was younger, I lived as a hobo for years, traversing North America. In those days, my closest companions were "friends from low places"—in the "Dirty South", in urban jungles, in the enchanting Southwest, in Lakota country. All the while, no harm came to me. I've been in jail twice for vagabondery—once in Surrey County, North Carolina, and a second time in Albuquerque, New Mexico...where I got to experience a riot squad. And I've had peaceable but intense run-ins with police in Romania, Transnistria, and Ukraine. I've been in the U.S. army and have made the acquaintance of military police. I'm a recovering/recovered addict and co-addict with over a decade of recovery. Just because I have glasses, and am "quiet" (I don't like to speak), doesn't mean I'm "nice." Phooey! I strive to be a good person. But I am not "nice." Yuck! I'm basically a former convenience store clerk and recovering addict who bears some interest in Humane Wisdom and the Threefold Idea.

Another thing: I've noticed that some liberal/progressive friends take a strange pleasure in magnifying the horror stories of U.S. prisons, and letting their imagination run wild—which has the side effect of watering their own fear and dread. I don't deny that prison is a place where one's karma, or the shared karma of our fallen humanity, could arrange for encountering the Living Hell. Yet having had various peaceable experiences with police and jails, much of what I've witnessed is the bland, bureaucratic, boring variety of evil, moreso than the outright lurid abuse as portrayed in films and television, and magnified by news reports. Though I am sorrowful that such abuse does occur, and though I see the systemic harmfulness of the Prison-Industrial Complex as well as anyone, my view is that most guards are ordinary people who are there to do an adequate job. And much of the prison system is run with as much professionalism as any other government agency, such as the U.S. post office, state school boards, or the DMV. I mean, a huge portion of populace is in jail or prison, and many, many ordinary people and activists have done time, without direct harm coming to them. Are liberals and Anthroposophists supposed to be more afraid of prison than ordinary citizens? If any of you do go to prison (which I wouldn't wish for), it is very likely you'll be fine.

As to the question some have asked: am I on the National Security Administration watch list? Perhaps. Perhaps not. I don't worry about it. My public writings and private aspirations are congruent. I am pretty open about my personal failings and historic weaknesses. I'm not a saint (duh!). All my thoughts and actions will be shouted from the rooftops under some sun anyway...and so will those of my adversary and those who are serving it.

As far as my worklife: at the place where I work as a janitor, the managers kindly facilitated my return without any hiccup.

Some weeks after my return, it was healing for me to go to an event at the Movement for Religious Renewal where the *Bidder 70* film about Tim DeChristopher (a fellow West Virginian) was shown. There were a couple men at the congregation who had been in jail or military prison for civil resistance—it was good to hear their experiences.

Also, since my release, I've been privileged to visit the local prisons in Hudson and Coxsackie as a member of our local singing group (we sing traditional New England shapenote songs and World Music). It has been wonderful to be with such noble friends as we intentionally step into that world and leave some hearty music to reverberate after our passing.

Lastly, someone said to me that though my action may not appear to have much outer effect in the world yet, it was like a dose of meteoric iron.

Takeaways:

I don't especially relish anyone being in jail, including myself. Though I did it with intention, this saga arose at a particular moment, in relation to Thoreau, to Occupy, and above all, to the idea of putting at least one Threefold Republic on the map of the world in our lifetime, in our century. There is one thing standing in the way: the Global Americanist Way.

And I've gotten to see the limits of "Anthroposophy-as-it-Exists." It is presently a rather tiny, sectarian-ish fellowship, and has forgotten its own prophecies, or interprets them in the most predictably vague and fuzzy way. Over the past couple years, my relationship with Anthroposophy-as-it-Exists reached a conclusion. Frankly, my interest is channeled into a new version of Humanosophy which has jettisoned whatever is hindering it from really becoming humanity's very most strongest, most Christic, most humane way of life. A Humane Way.

Lastly, I would have liked to have thanked each person who sent a letter, email, or silent thought, or was supportive in other ways. Till today, I'd never got around to simply thanking everyone. So...thank you!...and Happy Thanksgiving!

—Travis H.

P.S. Here are some kindly words written by others which touch on my effort:

▼ The Institute for Societal Holism wrote a letter "In Solidarity with Travis Henry": http://instituteforsocietalholism.tumblr.com/post/50928487203/in-solidarity-with-travis-henry

▼ The editor of the local Anthroposophic branch newsletter wrote: "Travis Henry and Civil Disobedience": www.berkshiretaconicbranch.org/resources/December-2012print.pdf

▼ Have Seeds Will Travel (based in Atlanta and Los Angeles) visited me afterward and wrote an interview:
https://haveseedswilltravel.org/category/travis-henry

▼ An artist in Texas wrote an Art and Anthroposophy blog entry: "Three Fold Now":
https://artandanthroposophy.wordpress.com/2014/01

P.P.S. And here is my Patreon site where I post updates in the long(?) path from here to the Threefold Republic:
https://www.patreon.com/henryt

"The Threefold Republic is completely done for in this century. It cannot become a reality. It will again be possible at the beginning of the coming century when a window of the spiritual world will open in order to make it possible."

—Rudolf S.

the second coming and the twelve step fellowships

Obviously the outward turning point of our century—the Threefold Republic—hasn't been enacted yet. Yet I offer my nascent research in regard to the inward turning point—the Second Coming. I can only give a fragmentary overview at this time. The identification of the Second Coming—the most significant event in two thousand years—is another crucial story which is presently perceived in anthroposophic circles in a blurry way. I mention this because it relates to the outward Culmination. How could the Second Coming in the 1930s not be closely related to the Culmination prophesied for the beginning of the 21st century?

In a previous essay, I have spoken of the Michaël Thought: namely, that the prophesied Culmination must be outwardly expressed by a full-fledged Threefold Republic, the Foothold of the Christ Impulse. And so it would be slippery of me to try to quietly skip over another prophecy relating to the Threefold Idea which, at first glance, appears not to have come true. In 1919, Rudolf Steiner is reported to have publically stated:

"The Threefold Republic is coming. **In about fifteen to twenty years** *it will be there. But then it will come in the midst of many catastrophes."*

> —Rudolf St., reported by Friedrich Rittelmeyer, co-founder of the Movement for Religious Renewal
> from Rittelmeyer's book *Rudolf Steiner Enters My Life*

Obviously, no Threefold Republic came around 1934 to 1939. Otherwise you would see it on the globe. Many catastrophes came, but no leaders arose to put a Threefold Republic on the map. Anthroposophy and the Federation for Trisecting the Social Organism *(Bund für Dreigliederung des sozialen Organismus)* were crafted to be as vigorously healing as National Socialism was vigorously destructive. But that original intention—a human intention and an intention of the spiritual world (God)—didn't manifest and touch ground. It would have been good if there had been enough anthroposophists and Waldorf people with the clarity, imagination, and cooperative will to at least have made a last-ditch effort. Even if they had failed laughably or terribly, the effort would have shone as a beacon for aftercomers, in a similar way that the White Rose continues to serve as a poignant beacon for the Democratic Republic.

"Had Germany accepted the message of the Threefold movement, there would never have been Hitlerism."

> —Ehrenfried Pfeiffer

Should we, in this case, view the "Coming of the Threefold Republic in the 1930s" prophecy as a wanhope and a wishful prayer of Rudolf Steiner's—an unheeded call—moreso than as an objective perception? No—my perspective is that Rudolf Steiner was perceiving the approach of God. But God and the gods won't arrange for things when human beings don't stand up and meet the spiritual world halfway.

However, as the primary prophet of humanity in the 20th century, surely Rudolf Steiner's prayerful vision of the Threefold Republic approaching in the mid-to-late-1930s must have shimmered into earthly reality in some way. My view is that Rudolf Steiner *was* perceiving the approach of the Kingdom of Heaven, but that it coalesced differently than how it looked as in spirit vision (thought). My perspective is that the Holy Spirit partially fulfilled Rudolf Steiner's "1930s Threefold Republic prophecy" through a working which resulted not in a Threefold Republic, but, rather, another social body.

Rudolf Steiner's dating of the Second Coming:

Notably, Rudolf Steiner designated roughly the same time period for the arrival of the Second Coming as he does for the prophesied (first)[34] arrival of the Threefold Republic.

---

[34] Dr. S's second prophecy and call for a Threefold Republic—to be enacted in the 21st century—is the subject of the first essay in this book: "Remarks on the Introduction of a Spiritual Empire."

*"The first indications of these new faculties will be noticeable in **isolated souls** comparatively soon now, and they will become more clearly apparent in the middle of the thirties of this century, **approximately in the period between 1930 and 1940. The years 1933, 1935 and 1937** will be particularly important."*

—Rudolf St., "The Reappearance of Christ in the Etheric", Lecture 1

*"As human beings become capable of seeing the etheric body, they will learn to see the etheric body of Christ Jesus, even as Paul saw it. This is what is beginning as the characteristic of a new age, and it will become manifest **between 1930 and 1940 to 1945** in the first forerunners among human beings who have these faculties. If human beings are attentive, they will experience this event of Damascus through direct spiritual observation, and with it clarity and truth about the Christ event."*

—Rudolf St. "The Reappearance of the Christ in the Etheric", Lecture 5

The prophecy of the first Threefold Republic was for "about 1934 to 1939." Similarly, the prophecy of the Second Coming is for "approximately 1930 to 1945." As far as the "isolated souls" spoken of by Rudolf Steiner, the word *isolated* could hardly be a more fitting description of those human souls who have fallen into active affliction.

The arrival of the Akronian Mysteries in 1934/1935:

I offer that 80 years ago, the Living Power leaped down to more deeply penetrate the human story, and has been quietly proclaiming and replicating Himself in necessary secrecy, through individual human willingness. To put it plainly: is it foolish to suggest that the most prominent Damascus Experience occurred on the island of Manhattan at 293 Central Park West, on or about the night of December 14th, in the year 1934? And furthermore, that this Power was first embodied socially on June 10th, 1935, in the city of Akron, Ohio, within the North American heartland? Am I a fool for voicing that the "group conscience" of these "Akronian Mysteries" are the first and primary embodiment of the Second Coming of the Representative of Humanity?

What I'm speaking of lies outside of anthroposophic waters, so I realize I may be losing readers with every word. Hardly any anthroposophists can yet tell the qualitative difference between the Akronian Mysteries and any other non-anthroposophical, outside stream (i.e. "threat"), such as Moon's Unification Church, Jehovah's Witnesses, or Mormons. However, any Michaël Path which aims to unfold in our century must seriously reckon with the most elementary, widespread initiatory path in our time.

What *did* come in 1935 is the Fellowship of Alcoholics Anonymous. In AA tradition, 1935 is known as Year Zero.

I mention all this not to provoke controversy, but for three reasons:

1) To address Rudolf Steiner's prophecy of a Threefold Social Organism coming between 1934 and 1939.
2) To assert that the Twelve Step recovery experience is, as yet, the primary embodiment of the Second Coming.
3) To point out that the crafting of any Michaël Path at this time, must take serious account of the Twelve Steps as the most widespread initiatory vehicle in our century.

Three Legacies came instead of the Threefold Republic:

Instead of a Threefold Republic, we have the Three Legacies of AA, a set of "3x12" principles. The Three Legacies are

- ▼ The Twelve Steps for Personal Recovery,
- ▼ The Twelve Traditions for Group Unity, and
- ▼ The Twelve Concepts for World Service.

This "3x12" social body did come in the midst of catastrophes. In AA's own words:

*"In our own times, we have seen millions die in **political and economic wars** often spurred by **religious and racial [cultural] difference**. We live in the imminent possibility of a fresh holocaust to determine how men shall be governed, and how the products of nature and toil shall be divided among them. This is the spiritual climate into which A.A. was born, and by God's grace has nevertheless flourished."*

I offer that because anthroposophists (whether they be Central European, Western, or Eastern European anthroposophists) were not willing or able to effectively stand up to any of the three heads of the National-State Beast—National Socialist, State Socialist, and Anglo-American Corporatist—and bring the Threefold Republic to the world stage during the 1930s, that a large portion of humanity's wellspring of healing forces was diverted into what manifest as the Fellowship of Alcoholics Anonymous and its Three Legacies.

So, for those who are not familiar with "the Rooms", here's an overview of what transpires:

Perception of the Etheric/Angelic World:

The Akronian Mysteries enable one to conceive one's own personal Higher Power, which then effectively steers the will onward to health. Since conceiving is perceiving, these are individuated *perceptions* of the non-physical, etheric world, the World of Life. Practically speaking, this conscious contact begins with the guardian angel, which is the personalized expression of the Representative of Humanity. With this contact comes awareness of synchronicity and serendipity. Higher Power is also heard through the voice of other human beings, which is a perception of others' angelic Higher Self. Thus the Intellectual Soul transitions to the Consciousness Soul, that is, conscious contact with spiritual realities.

From fused affliction to a threefold unfolding of the soul:

Among other things, in these Rooms a person learns to perceive the difference between their thoughts, their feelings, and their actions, and between spirit, emotion, and matter. Because each affliction is itself threefold—*obsession* in the thoughts, *craving* in the feelings, and *compulsion* in the will—the solution must be threefold as well: conceptual, psychic, and volitional. The 12 Step literature is pervaded with this threefold distinction. For example:

*"What is alcoholism? A.A.s see it as an illness, not a moral failing; as a progressive illness, which worsens as drinking continues; as an incurable, **threefold illness: physical, mental, and spiritual** which can be arrested by practicing the A.A. program."*

—Alcoholics Anonymous, "Speaking at Non-A.A. Meetings"

*"OA members have come to recognize that the disease of compulsive eating is **threefold: physical, emotional and spiritual**."*

—Overeaters Anonymous, "Treatment and Beyond"

Morning stars are rising:

As the result of traversing these volitional Steps: our Luciferian angelos (called "my addict" or "tiger") gets to return to their home in the Venus realm—where they continue their own evolution, and keep doing their own work (it's called "push-ups" in 12-Step speak), without interfering in our human soul.

*"So we have the prophetic word made more sure, and you are doing well in paying attention to it as to a lamp shining in a dark place—until day dawns and **a morning star rises in your hearts**."*

—Saint Peter's Second Letter

The Luciferian angelos no longer interferes, because their work is done, at least in regard to that affliction (that particular soul sheath)—as long as the human being remains in fit spiritual-volitional condition. Their human aspect did the excruciating work of climbing out of the mire, thereby reshaping their insides to the extent that the human being is much stronger than they were before they fell in. Thank you Lucifer! This could also be described as the transformation of astrality into Spirit Self, which is the Angelic component of a human being.

Rudolf Steiner speaks of recovery of the lucifers in this way:

*"What will happen in the future? Because with the help of Christ, **and with his help only,** you can **extinguish those qualities in you that stem from Lucifer**, you gradually **release the Luciferian powers** too. A time will come when the Luciferian powers, which had to sink to a lower stage of evolution for the sake of your freedom and therefore were unable*

*to experience the Christ Power on earth, will experience the Christ Power through you and be redeemed. You will redeem Lucifer if you receive the Christ Power in the appropriate way and, as a result, **you will grow stronger than you would otherwise have been**. For imagine, if you had not received the Luciferian forces, the Christ Power would have rayed out but would not have encountered any Luciferian obstacles. It would have been impossible for you to progress in goodness, truth and wisdom as far as you now can by having to overcome the powers of hindrance."*

—Rudolf St., "The Spiritual Hierarchies: Their Reflection in the Physical World"
(In this quotation, the words "we" and "humanity" are refreshed with "you.")

Lucifer's angelic comrades—the tigers in us—are waiting and longing for us to take the steps necessary for them to go home. Then our tigers will be doing 'push ups' elsewhere, in their home, the morning star. And we become at home in earth, which is our legitimate home.

That is what happens in the Rooms.

"So long as you have not lived this:
To die is to become new,
You remain a gloomy guest
On the dark earth."

—Johann Wolfgang von Goethe, *West-Eastern Divan*

It may be noted that because they come at affliction from the "other direction", so to speak, the co-afflictive fellowships such as Al-Anon Family Groups, have especially honed the mysteries of transforming the more subtle, but perhaps even more widespread curse of controloholism which is the Mephistophelean analog.

Recovery is a Near-Death Experience...the Lazarus Experience:

When Anthroposophists try to find evidence for the Second Coming, often the focus is on reports from physical near-death experiences. Yet this overlooks how since 1935, thousands of human beings, in the most grave and wretched conditions, are coming back from serious soul-death experiences. The Steps are a clearly transmittable path for the two experiences of dying and coming back.

I am not saying that the Near-Death Experiences and other spectacular visions of Christ which are usually pointed to in anthroposophic circles are unrelated to the Second Coming. I acknowledge them as significant outliers of the Second Coming, but outliers nonetheless. Why? Because their fruits are still especially unripe. What are the fruits of the NDEs as a whole? Have the NDEs resulted in a NDE fellowship which brings people back from affliction and soul death? Have the NDEs resulted in an independent NDE primary and secondary school system, NDE curative communities, NDE organic farms, or NDE statecraft? Have the NDEs resulted in a replicable and transmittable path of personal and civilizational renewal? No. And yet...the Representative of Humanity comes in a social body.

Also Anthroposophists' focus on NDEs betrays a somewhat materialistic bent—because in the eyes of NDE watchers, only physical death "counts." Whereas, the Twelve Steppers in every corner of North America (and many foreign lands) are returning to life after having almost died soulwise, rather than physically. No one enters the Rooms because their life is happy-go-lucky. The human being is at the end of their rope, at the bottom of the U, at the last stop on the line, very close to "jails, institutions, and death."...And then they come back to life within the Rooms of the Akronian Mysteries. That is the primary Lazarus Experience of our time. It is being enacted literally in nearly every neighborhood and village in North America. The usual setting for this drama is the modern catacomb—the basement or back room of some church or synagogue or community center. Because the Rooms are anonymous and confidential, this happens off the edge of the public consciousness. But it is there.

*"When this **powerlessness is experienced with sufficient intensity**, there comes **the sudden reversal**, the other experience, which tells us that if we do not merely depend on what our bodily forces enable us to achieve, but devote ourselves to what the spirit gives, then we can overcome this **inner death of the soul**. [...] A person who can say not merely that he feels the Divine within him, as mystical theosophists eloquently assert, but can speak of the **two experiences—that of powerlessness** and **that of the resurrection from it**—such a person is speaking of **the true Christ-experience**. [...] Truly*

*there is no need today to despair of **finding the Christ in immediate experience,** for He has been found in very truth when a person has rediscovered his own true being—but **always after the realization of powerlessness.**"*

—Maria Krehbiel-Darmstädter,
An anthroposophist and Christian Community member who perished in the Auschwitz Concentration Camp in 1943.

The Akronian Mysteries are specific:

Please note that I am speaking about the Twelve Step Fellowships specifically—not about the "self help" movement in general. "Self-help group" is an outside term; Twelve Steppers generally don't refer to the Fellowships by that term; rather, these are "God help" or "mutual help" fellowships. To lump the Fellowships with the kaleidoscope of dubious self-help groups would be like not being able to distinguish Anthroposophy from any other "occult group" or New Age group. The 12 Step Movement and the Anthropsophic Movement are very specific movements with specific, concrete formative potentials.

The Akronian Mysteries are pervasive:

For example, in my rural Columbia County in Upstate New York, there are 35 AA meetings per week. Even the small villages typically have an AA meeting. In the county seat of Hudson, there are multiple meetings on every day of the week. In this county there are also 4 NA meetings, one Al-Anon meeting, one Adult Children of Alcoholics/Dysfunctional Families meeting, an OA meeting, an SA meeting, one Celebrate Recovery (Christian 12 step) meeting, and a Clutterers Anonymous meeting. All of these fellowships are explicitly centered on the Twelve Steps of AA.

Even in the sparsely-populated county where I grew up in West Virginia, there are currently 17 AA meetings, 10 NA meetings, and two Al-Anon meetings.

Why don't you choose your own conception of God?:

It may be noted that when a hopelessly afflicted person has returned to life via enacting the Twelve Steps, then the Living Christ is has gotten a handhold into their will and sentient body, regardless of what name they call Him. In the Akronian Mysteries, God is humble enough to respond to any name. It's a mystical fact. There is no other source of the light in their eyes. No one comes to the Father except through Him...even if we didn't know who we were going to, or coming through. Volition (willingness) takes precedence over theology (conception).

The most crucial words in the founding of the Akronian Mysteries are these:

"Why don't you choose your own conception of God?"

Those were the words that evoked the scales to fall from Bill W's eyes. Those words are so crucial, that this is one moment in the 20th century when the Representative of Humanity Himself somehow spoke through the words of another man. In November of 1934, Bill W...a hopeless drunkard...was visited by an old drinking buddy who had miraculously recovered via enacting the Oxford Group's six steps.[35] This is how the story goes:

*"My friend suggested what then seemed a novel idea. He said, **"Why don't you choose your own conception of God?"** That statement hit me hard. It melted the icy intellectual mountain in whose shadow I had lived and shivered many years. I stood in the sunlight at last.*
*[...] **Scales of pride and prejudice fell from my eyes.** A new world came into view."*

This affirms that the Second Coming must be based on a pluri-religious approach to the Representative of Humanity.[36] The 12 Step Fellowships are a poignant model of practical inter-religious, inter-philosophical harmony. Anthroposophy bears

---

[35] The Oxford Group was the main predecessor of Alcoholics Anonymous, in a similar way the Theosophical Society preceded the Anthroposophic Society.

[36] For more, see "My Politics and Religion Article in LILIPOH Magazine" and "A Pluri-religious Movement for Renewal": www.patreon.com/posts/my-politics-and-5373999
https://sites.google.com/site/4religiousrenewal

the singular responsibility to provide a conceptual foundation for the Second Coming—not so much to inculcate a sectarian, anthroposophically-flavored Cosmic Christ as the only true Higher Power—but rather to deftly inform spiritual wayfarers of the seemingly paradoxical "Trans-Christian Christology" which spiritual science perceives, whereby all religions and philosophies (even secular philosophy) have their origin in the Light of the World, who walked the earth as a human being at the turning point of humanity's story. It is also vital to point out that the historic misapplication of Jesus' name is an etheric-conceptual, mephistophelean imposter of Christ, known as Bar-Jesus, the "evil Jesus."

Anyone who has taken the steps to recover their spiritual-volitional fitness has the Christic Power in them. Christ Jesus is the first human being to recover from all afflictions—including death—and so He is the archetype and power source for any subsequent human recoveries, regardless of in which religious or non-religious context they occur. But it would be a serious mistake to read references to "Christ" in a way that infers that anyone gets a bonus star for being a card-carrying Christian. The goal now is to permeate all religions and worldviews with 12-Step-enhanced Christic volition, and with anthroposophically-enhanced Christological understanding, while lovingly preserving and furthering each tradition's aesthetic and humane treasures.

Here is a medley of quotes from the Fellowships and from Anthroposophy which affirm the pluri-religious character of the Christic Power, who views all religions as trees in the same orchard.

*"Social distinctions, petty rivalries and jealousies—these are laughed out of countenance. Being wrecked in the same vessel, being restored and **united under one God**, with hearts and minds attuned to the welfare of others, the things which matter so much to some people no longer signify much to them. How could they?"*

—Bill W, "A Vision for You", AA Big Book

"As a society we must never become so vain as to suppose that we are authors of a new religion. We will humbly reflect that every one of AA's principles was borrowed from ancient sources. [...] By personal religious affiliation, we include Catholics, Protestants, Jews, Hindus, and a sprinkling of Moslems and Buddhists."
—Bill W, *As Bill Sees It*

"Goethe's poem, Die Geheimnisse *("The Mysteries")...expresses the ideal of the Rosicrucians. According to the explanation given by Goethe to certain students, **each of the twelve Companions of the Rose Cross represents a religious creed.**"*

—Rudolf St., "An Esoteric Cosmology"

*"Thus gradually there develops the higher man, the representative of humanity, the chosen one, who works as the Thirteenth here, in the society of the Twelve, the great secret Brotherhood which, under the sign of the Rose-Cross has taken upon itself for all of humanity **the mission of harmonizing the religions scattered in the world.**"*

—Rudolf St., "The Mysteries"

*"The **greatest harm has always come to humanity** [...] **from exclusivity,** with Christianity opposed to Buddhism, Judaism, and all other religions."*

—Rudolf St., "One Fire, Many Tongues"

*"If we are to fare well in the Sun sphere between death and the new birth, it is essential to be able to understand not merely one particular group of human beings but to **understand and find points of contact with all human souls.** In the Sun sphere we feel isolated, like hermits, **if the prejudices of one particular faith render us incapable of understanding a human being whose soul has been filled with the principles of a different faith.** An individual who on the Earth regarded one particular religion only as valuable is incapable in the Sun sphere of **understanding adherents of other religions.** But the consequences of this lack of understanding are not the same as they are on Earth. On the Earth men may live side by side without any inner understanding of each other and then separate into different faiths and systems of thought. In the Sun sphere, however, since we interpenetrate one another, we are together and yet at the same time separated in our inner being; and in that sphere every separation and every lack of understanding are at once sources of terrible suffering.*

Every contact with an adherent of a different faith becomes a reproach which weighs upon us unceasingly and which we cannot escape because **on Earth we did not educate ourselves in this respect.**"

—Rudolf St., "Between Death and Rebirth"

"The teachings given to humanity in Christianity are so profound, so full of wisdom, that no religion of the future will be able to displace or supplant Christianity. It will be possible for **Christianity to adapt itself to all the forms of civilization** in the future."

—Rudolf St., "The Gospel of John" lecture, Basel

"When human beings actually reach that heavenly language which expresses the significance of the various religious Founders and Inspirers of humanity, then will the Anthroposophical ideal of a tolerant and unbiased **consideration of all religions and cosmic conceptions** be really able to appear. Human beings will no longer quarrel when they no longer claim for their own group a particular bearer of religion or stream of civilization, but seek for the origin of these bearers outside in cosmic space. In this sense **such a contemplation may acquire great moral importance** if in much which formerly brought divisions and disharmonies upon earth, peace and harmony are established."

—Rudolf St., "The Spiritual Beings in the Heavenly Bodies and in the Kingdoms of Nature"

"Love is higher than opinion. If people love one another, the most varied opinions can be reconciled. Hence it is deeply significant that in Theosophy **no religion is attacked and no religion is specially singled out, but all are understood**, and so there can be siblinghood because the **adherents of the most varied religions understand one another.** This is one of the most important tasks for humanity today and in the future: that human beings should learn to live together and understand one another. If this human fellowship is not achieved, all talk of occult development is empty."

—Rudolf St., "At the Gates of Spiritual Science", Lecture 11; "Brotherhood" is here refreshed as "siblinghood."

"The bestowal on humanity of **complete freedom in the religious life**—this underlies the impulses, at least, of the work of the Angels."

—Rudolf St., "The Work of the Angels in the Human Beings's Astral Body"

Defining the relation of Anthroposophy to the different faiths in Basel in 1917, Rudolf Steiner. stated that:

"There is no clash between anthroposophy and **any man's religious faith.** It is impossible to convert anthroposophy directly into religion. But anthroposophy, genuinely understood, will create a genuine, true, unfeigned religious need. For the human soul **needs various paths** to direct it on the way upwards to its goal. The human soul needs not only the power conferred by knowledge, it must be penetrated by the warmth that comes from the kind of contemplation of the spiritual world that is peculiar to religious faith, to true religious feeling."

In that same year Rudolf Steiner spoke on the same subject in Berlin:

"We should never behave as if the quest for spiritual knowledge were a substitute for the practice of religion and religious life. Spiritual knowledge can greatly sustain religious life and the practice of religion, particularly in regard to the mystery of Christ; but we should be perfectly clear that religious life and the practice of religion within the human community kindles the spiritual consciousness of the soul. If this spiritual consciousness is to come alive in man, he cannot remain content with abstract representations of God or Christ but will have to involve himself again and again in the practice of religion, in religious activity, **which for each individual can take on a different form.**"

Words from others:

"Goal: To bring about true Christianity and **the synthesis of all religions**"

—Ehrenfried Pfeiffer, in regard to the meeting of the leadership of humanity in 1250 AD, from his "Chart of the History of Mankind"

"There is no religion that is not Christianity."

—Novalis

These words strongly affirm that the Twelve Step Fellowships and Anthroposophy bear—or could bear—an especially pluralistic, yet vigorously articulated formative power: a "trans-Christian" Christic theology and volition. In this way, these two vanguards of the Second Coming begin to restore the shared understanding of a Higher Power which existed among ancient humanity:

*"The identical thing that we now call **the Christian religion existed among the ancients** and has not been lacking from the beginnings of the human race until **the coming of Christ in the flesh**, from which moment on the true religion, **which already existed**, began to be called Christian."*

—Saint Augustine

The hot flash—Bill's Damascus Experience:

Soon after that conversation, Bill was hospitalized. The "boost" from his friend's visit wore off and that night, Bill's feeling of despair deepened. As distress mounted, Bill said to himself:

"I'll do anything, anything at all! If there be a God, let Him show Himself!"

"What happened next was electric. Suddenly, my room blazed with an indescribably white light. I was seized with an ecstasy beyond description. Every joy I had known was pale by comparison. The light, the ecstasy—I was conscious of nothing else for a time.

"Then, seen in the mind's eye, there was a mountain. I stood upon its summit, where a great wind blew. A wind, not of air, but of spirit. In great, clean strength, it blew right through me. Then came the blazing thought, "You are a free man." I know not at all how long I remained in this state, but finally the light and the ecstasy subsided. I again saw the wall of my room. As I became more quiet, a great peace stole over me, and this was accompanied by a sensation difficult to describe. I became acutely conscious of a Presence, which seemed like a veritable sea of living spirit. I lay on the shores of a new world."

—Bill W, *Pass It On*

There is the Damascus Experience which sparked the Second Coming.

In humanity's story, the site where Bill experienced the "hot flash" on or about the night of December 14th, in the year 1934, is parallel or equivalent to the spot on the road to Damascus, Syria where Saul was blinded. That spot is 293 Central Park West, on the island of Manhattan, here in the State of New York.

The Second Coming must have social fruits:

If Bill W had simply pocketed his 'hot flash' and went on with his newly sober life, that would be one more nice story to add to the Near Death Experience scrapbook.

But no, he strongly sensed that if he did not transmit his experience, that it would leave him. The following May, 1935, he was on a business trip in Akron, Ohio, and the craving started to return. He frantically called a local church to see if there were any drunks he could share his story with. The church connected him with a hopeless alcoholic named Bob Smith, who happened to be a medical doctor. Long story short, Dr. Bob and Bill W connected, and Dr. Bob became permanently sober on June 10th, 1935—the date which is celebrated as foundation of the Fellowship of Alcoholics Anonymous. A Fellowship doesn't exist unless there are two people.

This date could be considered to be the start of the Second Coming, in a similar way the First Coming began on April 3rd, 33 A.D, with the completion of the Mystery of Golgotha, and the earthly birth of the Higher Power of Humanity.

The Akronian Mysteries are an intersection of higher power and human agency:

In contrast to being run over by a truck, the 12 Step Lazarus Experience is based on a balance between human agency and receptivity to higher power. There's a saying in the Rooms: *"Without God, I can't. With me, God won't."*

The Recovery Mysteries regard the human being as *"intelligent agents, spearheads of God's ever advancing Creation."* (Big Book p.85)

The Akronian Mysteries are adaptable to various afflictions:
The Three Legacies have been adapted by subsequent fellowships of the ever-expanding Twelve Step Movement, thereby permeating into many spheres of suffering. These are the Fellowships I know of which are based on the 12 Steps (along with a few "special composition" associations explicitly affiliated with AA):

Fellowships dealing with All Afflictions:
All Addictions Anonymous (AAA)
All Addicts Anonymous (AAA)
Recovery Anonymous (RA)

Substance Use:
Alcoholics Anonymous (AA)
Chemically Dependent Anonymous (CDA)
Cocaine Anonymous (CA)
Crystal Meth Anonymous (CMA)
Drug Addicts Anonymous (DAA)
Heroin Anonymous (HA)
Marijuana Anonymous (MA)
Narcotics Anonymous (NA)
Nicotine Anonymous (NicA)
Pills Anonymous (PA)

Co-Affliction and Individuation (related to a family or friend's substance use, general family dysfunction, and criminal socialization):
Adult Children of Alcoholics/Dysfunctional Families (ACA/ACoA)
Alateen
Al-Anon Family Groups
Co-Anon Family Groups (CA's co-afflictive fellowship)
Co-Ateen
Co-Dependents Anonymous (CoDA)
Criminals and Gang Members Anonymous (CGA)
Families Anonymous (FA)
Gangsters Anonymous (GA)
Nar-Anon Family Groups
Narateen
Pil-Anon Family Program

Food and Eating:
Anorexics & Bulimics Anonymous (ABA)
Compulsive Eaters Anonymous-HOW (CEA-HOW)
Eating Disorders Anonymous (EDA)
Food Addicts Anonymous (FAA)
Food Addicts in Recovery Anonymous (FA)
GreySheeters Anonymous (GSA)
O-Anon Family Groups
Overeaters Anonymous (OA)

Sexuality and Relationship:
Chapter Nine—Couples in Recovery Anonymous
COSA (co-afflictive counterpart to SAA)
Co-Sex and Love Addicts Anonymous (COSLAA)
Divorce Anonymous (DA)
Incest Survivors Anonymous (ISA)
Love Addicts Anonymous (LAA)
Recovering Couples Anonymous (RCA)
Recovery in the Lifestyle (RitL)
Relationships Anonymous (RA)
SA-Couples
S-Anon International Family Groups
S-Ateen
Sex Addicts Anonymous (SAA)
Sex and Love Addicts Anonymous (SLAA)
Sex Workers Anonymous (SWA)
Sexaholics Anonymous (SA)
Sexual Compulsives Anonymous (SCA)
Sexual Recovery Anonymous (SRA)
Singles Anonymous (SA)
SRA-Anon
Survivors of Incest Anonymous (SIA)
SWAN (SWA's co-afflictive fellowship)

Emotional Recovery:
Affective Disorders Anonymous (ADA)
Anxiety Anonymous
Depressed Anonyomous (DepA)
Double Trouble in Recovery (DTR)
Dual Diagnosis Anonymous (DDA)
Dual Disorders Anonymous (DDA)
Dual Recovery Anonymous (DRA)
Emotional Health Anonymous
Emotions Anonymous (EA)
Everyone's Recovery Groups (ERG)
Neurotics Anonymous (N/A)
Obsessive Compulsive Anonymous (OCA)
Obsessive Skin-Pickers Anonymous (OSPA)
Post-Traumatic Stress Disorder Anonymous (PTSDA)
Rageaholics Anonymous (RA)
Self-Mutilators Anonymous (SMA)
Social Phobics Anonymous/Social Anxiety Anonymous (SP/SocAA)

Religion-based 12 Step Fellowships:
Adventist Recovery Ministries (ARMin)
Alcoholics for Christ (A/C)
Alcoholics Victorious (AV)
Buddhist Recovery Network (BRN)
Calix Society (Not based on the 12 Steps, but was explicitly formed to be a Catholic complement to membership in AA.)
Celebrate Recovery (CR)
Celebrate Freedom (CF)
Jewish Alcoholics, Chemically Dependent Persons and Significant Others (JACS)
LDS Addiction Recovery Program
Millati Islami (Islamic adaptation of the 12 Steps as the "Path of Peace")
Overcomers Outreach (OO)
Pagan ODAT

Profession-based 12 Step and AA professional groups:
Bird of a Feather (BOAF): Pilots in AA
Caduceus Club
International Doctors in Alcoholics Anonymous (IDAA)
International Lawyers in A.A. (ILAA)

Culturally-based 12 Step Fellowships and AA associations
Grupo de Cuarto y Quinto Paso (CQ). (A Mexican-centered 12-Step Fellowship which features portraits of Bill and Bob and Jesus in their service.)

How to Recover from the Addiction to White Supremacy (A Pan African 12-Step Model for a Mental Health Peer Group)

Native American Indian General Service Office of Alcoholics Anonymous (NAIGSO-AA)

White Bison: Wellbreity Recovery Circles

Householding and Economic Recovery:
Clutterers Anonymous (CLA)
Debtors Anonymous (DA)
Gam-A-Teen
Gam-Anon Family Groups
Gamblers Anonymous (GA)
Oxford House
Shoplifters Anonymous (ShA)
Spenders Anonymous (SA)
Underearners Anonymous (UA)
Workaholics Anonymous (WA)

Other 12 Step fellowships and special composition associations of AA:
Artists Recovering Through the Twelve Steps (A.R.T.S.).

Association Recovering Motorcyclists (ARM) (along with many other 12-Step inspired motorcycle clubs)
Gays and Lesbians in Alcoholics Anonymous (GaL-AA)
Internet & Tech Addiction Anonymous (ITAA)
On-Line Gamers Anonymous (OLGA)

There also many 12 Step-based books by independent authors which adapt the principles to a particular situation or cultural stream, but which aren't yet embodied as a Fellowship. For example:

The Pagan in Recovery: The Twelve Steps from a Pagan Perspective, or

Yoga and the Twelve Step Path.

The Akronian Mysteries' relationship with civilizational streams:

As for existing institutions, the 12 Steps have been adopted, adapted, or referred to by the Catholic Church (the Calix Society), the Mormon Church (LDS Recovery Program), the Evangelical Movement (Celebrate Recovery and Alcoholics Victorious), the Seventh-day Adventists Recovery Ministries, the Salvation Army (some of the first Narcotics Anonymous meetings were formed in the context of the Salvation Army), and the US Navy (Navy MORE Program: "My Ongoing Recovery Experience", launched in 2010). Though most Fellowships are secular and inter-religious, the Fellowships of Alcoholics for Christ, Alcoholics Victorious, Celebrate Recovery, and Overcomers Outreach feature specifically Christian re-languaging of the 12 Steps. The Steps have also been adopted and adapted by Islamic, Jewish, Buddhist, and pagan recovery groups. As for secularism, there is a growing association of agnostic AA groups which apply the 12 Step principles from an entirely human-centered perspective. These Agnostic Groups are full members of the AA World Service Structure. What other spiritual pathway is endorsed by such diverse voices? The 12 Steps are endorsed because of their palpable fruits.

"A minister in Thailand wrote, "We took A.A.'s Twelve Steps to the largest Buddhist monastery in this province, and the head priest said, "Why, these Steps are fine! For us as Buddhists, it might be slightly more acceptable if you had inserted the word 'good' in your Steps instead of 'God.' Nevertheless, you say that it is God as you understand Him, and that must certainly include the good. Yes, A.A.'s Twelve Steps will surely be accepted by the Buddhists around here.'"

—Bill W, *As Bill Sees It*

"When I meet a Jewish person who is in active addiction, I do not offer them to go synagogue and pray. The first place I'm going to send them is to the appropriate 12-step group."

—Rabbi Shais Taub, of the Orthodox Jewish movement Chabad

When I worked in the Threefold Community, I became aware that one place one could freely interact with the surrounding Hasidic and orthodox Jewish community was via the Rooms.

"We will need to build an Islamically grounded 12-step culture."

—Mohammed Al-Turaiki, the Chief Executive of Saudi Care for Rehabilitation and Health Care, in Saudi Arabia, 2010

In the Islamic Republic of Iran, the Twelve Step Movement has rapidly replicated itself. In October of 1990, Narcotics Anonymous stepped into the heroin epidemic in Iran. The first NA Group was founded, as usual, by a couple of rag-tag recovered addicts. Fast forward 20 years, this is the result: In a 2012 report, of the 61,800 Narcotics Anonymous meetings worldwide, 27,650 were in the USA and 15,955 in the rest of the world...except for Iran. As of 2012, there were *18,195 weekly NA meetings in Iran.*[37] The Farsi-language translation of the NA Basic Text accounts for ¼ of all sales worldwide. More NA pamphlets are distributed yearly in Iran than the rest of the world combined.

The Fellowship has been designated by the Iranian Government as the country's favorite non-governmental entity. When the Iranian Government asked NA how the government might help the Fellowship, NA essentially said: "Stay out of our way." The Iranian Government could hardly believe that an NGO wasn't looking for government funding. The Twelve Steps have been lauded as embodying "Persian cultural values." Iranians speak of "the traditions of Persian culture that worked so well in conjunction with the 12 Steps and 12 Traditions of NA."

Can you imagine anthroposophy and societal trisecting making such inroads on a big scale, flowing seamlessly through all civilizations?

I can. But it will require an upgrading and metamorphosis.

The Three Legacies are not the Threefold Republic:

---

[37] —"The Crescent and the Needle: The Remarkable Rise of NA in Iran", April 2014
www.thefix.com/content/Iran-Narcotics-Anonymous-phonemoneon-Lavitt2099?page=all

So some might ask: If the Twelve Step Fellowships are the redirected fruitage of Threefold Impulse which was intended to manifest in the 1930s, then will the Fellowships and their Three Legacies somehow magically result in a Threefold Republic? No, they won't. Their singleness of purpose intentionally prevents that. Statecraft is not their purpose. And so, the Twelve Step Movement is proto-Michaëlic (in some ways "Dismasic"), but not yet Michaëlic. Even with the Twelve Traditions guarding its way, without the Threefold Republic, the 12 Step Movement will eventually fall to commercialism or governmentalism, if not in structure, then in tone. However, any Michaël Path which aims to unfold now must seriously reckon with the Twelve Steps, as the most widespread initiatory path of our century. And not for condescending reasons of making Anthroposophy more "accessible" to a wider audience. Rather, any such Michaël Path for the renewal of Humane Wisdom would be genuinely strengthened by fully tapping into the Three Legacies.

Anthroposophy is crucial, yet the spirit blows where it will:

When I have voiced the centrality of the 12 Step Impulse, I have experienced some strange responses from Anthroposophists. One said that surely this is an atavistic impulse—even a harmful movement—since these Mysteries rely on the power of a group, instead of overcoming affliction through one's own individual willpower and meditation. What that tells me is that this person has not yet consciously perceived what a fallen Archangel is, or the Luciferian double, and perceived its power relative to an un-enhanced human personality. Also, the person does not know, even with the presence of a group and the graceful serendipity of a higher power, what gigantic efforts of individual willingness are necessary to climb out of hell and to evoke a psychic change great enough to allow the Luciferian angelos to go home.

Are Anthroposophists' feelings hurt because the deepest initial impulse of the Kingdom of the Heaven didn't show up at the Goetheanum wearing a white suit? The spirit blows where it will.

Are Anthroposophists incredulous because the Second Coming didn't begin in Central Europe? But isn't North America just as accessible by the Holy Spirit as Switzerland? Every earthly distance is next door in the spiritual world. God and the gods will not be kept in a box.

The Akronian Mysteries are good, but incomplete...and the Anthroposophic Mysteries are wise, but incomplete:

Yes, from a whole-earth perspective, the Twelve Step Mysteries are one-sided. They came out of the American Continent, where our deepest concern is for health.

*"The ideal which proceeds from Western initiation is making human beings **healthy** and keeping them **healthy**, and giving humankind the possibility of **healthy** development. [...] The Westerner who approaches the Doorway [..] sees the spirits that permeate the world and humanity with **sickness** and death in the broadest sense, as injurious, destructive and degrading for humanity."*

—Rudolf St., "Social and Anti-Social Forces in the Human Being", 1918

Duh! That has been my experience. Health is actually our legitimate mission as Far Western humanity. The Akronian Mysteries are all about health. Step Two says: *"Came to believe a Power greater than myself could restore me to **sanity (health)**"*.

In contrast, the mission of Central European humanity is to overcome polarization via flexible, trinitarian, living thinking.

*"In the Central European countries **there is a middle condition of affairs.** [...] If you turn to the Central European people what will you find, when those who are being initiated are not taken out of their nation and raised to universal humanity, but when the Folk Spirit co-operates with them? Then the first important experience which comes to our notice is a conflict between those [Luciferian] spiritual beings who belong to higher worlds, to the other side of the Doorway, and certain other [Mephistophelean] beings who are here in the physical world, on this side of the Doorway but who are invisible to ordinary consciousness. The Central Europeans will first become aware of this conflict. The experience of this conflict makes itself felt to the genuine seeker after truth in the Central European countries as a being penetrated with **the powers of doubt**. One becomes acquainted with all **the powers of "many-sidedness".**"*

—Rudolf St., "Social and Anti-Social Forces in the Human Being", 1918

I strongly suggest that even though Rudolf Steiner himself pointed this out, the Anthroposophic Mysteries, as they exist, often lead people into shallow many-sidedness. Just because it's the "middle" doesn't mean it's complete...it's a shallow middle.

Without the Far Western Mysteries, the Anthroposophic Mysteries will become *too* flexible and many-sided—a hip and beautiful, but wishy-washy tradition whose will is lamed by doubt and flakiness.

And without the Anthroposophic Mysteries, the Akronian Mysteries will be limited to only fields of personal health, and will become conceptually flat and standardized. Furthermore, without anthroposophic enhancement, the Recovery Movement will not be able to penetrate into every sphere of life ("all our affairs.").[38]

The Second Coming is dramatic and visible:

Recently, an anthroposophist friend flatly asserted: *"The Second Coming was never meant to be an outwardly dramatic and visible event."*

Of course, it would crassly materialistic (satanic) to look for a physical man dropping down from the clouds in a parachute. But dramatic and visible? Yes, why wouldn't the Second Coming be as dramatic as the First Coming, or as dramatic as the founding of the other civilizational streams and turning points? Why wouldn't its living *effects* be perceivable in human beings, even at a large scale?

Consider the foundation of earlier mystery streams. Each of these events have a coherent, discernable story behind them, with human agents, and palpable effects:

- ▼ The foundation—according to anthroposophic legendry—of the Manuvian Mysteries in Central Asia by the Sun Oracle, over 10,000 years ago, which intentionally instilled intellect into a human language, and thus, into human consciousness. This was before the oceans fully condensed and fell. These qualities have since become the common heritage of humankind, of all language families.
- ▼ The foundation of the Vedic (Indian) Mysteries by the Seven Rishis in 7227 BC.
- ▼ The foundation of the Zoroastrian (Persian) Mysteries by the Original Zoroaster in 5067 BC.
- ▼ The foundation of the Adamite Mysteries by Oannes Adapa, the Second Adam, circa 4758 BC. Oannes brought civilizational renewal to Mesopotamian humanity, including the Semitic peoples. (The Original Adamite event, with which this Second Adamite event is artistically melded in the Mosaïc legendarium, occurred over 25,000 years ago, in the Mesozoic Age of the Lost World.)
- ▼ The foundation of the Noahide Mysteries in Mesopotamia by Noah and the seventy Noahide initiates, following a worldwide "zombie apocalypse" of deathly sleep which began 3102 BC, externally coinciding with local flooding. The Hebrew Noah is the same person as the Sumerian Ziusudra and the Assyrian Utnapishtim. The Noahide principles were propagated to all corners of the decimated earth. Even the far western branches of humanity in the American Continents were reached by a Noahide pioneer named Maniton, who is recorded in Armenian and Anishinaabe tradition. In the surviving national legends, the original Manuvian oceanic flood and this second Noachian soporific flood are usually artistically melded. All surviving pockets of humankind acknowledged the Noahide impulse as the legitimate pathway forward.
- ▼ The foundation of the Kemetic (Egyptian) Mysteries by Thoth (Hermes) in 2907 BC.

---

[38] Some might ask: then where are the Eastern Mysteries in Humane Way? Where is the third parent? Good question. The Eastern Mysteries are concerned with overcoming egotism. If I had to immediately choose a third leg for Humane Way, I would suggest the mindfulness practices as embodied in the Vietnamese Buddhism of Thich Nhat Hanh. However, at this point, it is not feasible to fully meld mindfulness practice with the Four Legacies, because there would need to be pre-existing sources for learning how to apply mindfulness in most or all of the Twelve Quests. I'm not aware that the mindfulness literature is widely-focused enought to cover that, or that the mindfulness practice centers are geographically pervasive enough to serve as the third "farm team" for Humane Way. However, the concept of Allied Ways allows for any and all of the Eastern Mysteries to engage with the Four Legacies. In that way, we can see what truly enhances the efficacy of the Four Legacies. In the further future—perhaps a generation or more away from now—there could be...and probably should be...the selection of a third, Eastern mainline "parent" for Humane Way. This would require a ¾ vote by all groups who are members of the World Service Assembly. Humane Way literature would need to be extensively revised to include examples from the third stream, alongside Recovery examples and Anthroposophic examples.

- ▼ The foundation of the Sinitic (Chinese) Mysteries by the Yellow Emperor, traditionally dated to 2698 BC, who is perhaps the Archangel Lucifer enfleshed, in a mostly positive sense. A one-sided continuation of the antediluvian mysteries of Nǚwā and Fúxī, and of the Original Tao.
- ▼ The foundation of the Sinaïc (Jewish) Mysteries by the Egyptian ex-priest Moses Osarseph and the Seventy Elders, traditionally dated at 1313 BC.
- ▼ The foundation of the Hibernian Mysteries by the druid Amergin, via the Milesian (Gaëlic) conquest of Ireland, traditionally dated to either 1700 BC or 1287 BC. A continuation of the pre-Noachian mystery centers.
- ▼ The foundation of the Brittonic Mysteries by Brutus of Troy, the first king of Britain, circa 1100 BC, as an offshoot of the Etruscan-Roman Mysteries.
- ▼ The foundation of the Nazarene Mysteries by Nazatharos (the Later Zoroaster) in Babylonia circa 600s BC, and thence borne by the Jewish People.
- ▼ The foundation of the Buddhadharmic Mysteries in 589 BC by Siddhartha Gautama, thence transmitted via the Ten Principle Disciples.
- ▼ The foundation of the Taoist Mysteries in 521 BC by Lǎozǐ, and the Confucian Mysteries in 519 BC by Kǒng Qiū. The two men cross paths in 518 BC. The Sinitic Mysteries split into a left-hand path and right-hand path.
- ▼ The foundation of the Northern Mysteries by Sig, a Scythian prince, in the first century BC. A penultimate renewal of the Odinic Mysteries which were founded in the mists of time.
- ▼ The foundation of the Christian Mysteries via the Twelve Apostles and the Great Commission of the 72 Disciples. Greek civilization metamorphoses into the Christian Church. The enactment of the Golgothan Mystery by the Representative of Humanity on April 3rd, 33 AD.
- ▼ The foundation of the Manichæan Mysteries by Mani (Latin name: Manes) in 240 AD.
- ▼ The foundation of the Arthurian Mysteries, initiated by Merlin Ambrosius, the Last of the Romans. A Christian continuation of the ancient Brittonic Mysteries. Through the death of Arthur in 537 AD, Celtic civilization morphs into Western esotericism.
- ▼ The foundation of the Islamic Mysteries by Muhammad and the Companions in 613 AD. Continues to serve as the legitimate rearguard of humanity and seal of the religions.
- ▼ The foundation of the Grail Mysteries in northern Spain by Titurel in the 800s AD.
- ▼ The foundation of the Chartresian Mysteries by Bishop Fulbert in 1006 AD.
- ▼ The foundation of the Rosicrucian Mysteries by Christian Rosenkreutz in 1413 AD.
- ▼ The foundation of the Scientistic Mysteries by Francis Bacon in 1605 AD, with the publication of his book *Proficience and Advancement of Learning* which inculcated the idea of scientistic progress. Hardly anyone, except for a few occultists, fully realize that the scientific worldview in which humanity is now immersed, and which is forcibly mandated by government agencies (such as public schools), is a particular sacerdotal-initiatory cultural matrix with specific benefits (which must be safeguarded) and biases (which must be surmounted). Scientism is not everything.
- ▼ The foundation of the Theosophical Mysteries by Helena Blavatsky in 1875.
- ▼ The foundation of the Anthroposophic Mysteries by Rudolf Steiner with the Participants in the Christmas Foundation Conference in 1923.

So all of these spiritual-physical events have actual human personalities and stories, but anthroposophists are saying that the Second Coming has no perceivable or coherent story behind it??? The SECOND COMING!!!

Nay, I offer that this is the story so far:

- ▼ The foundation of the Akronian Mysteries by Bill and Bob in 1935, and the First One-Hundred (actually 73 members by 1939). The first inner/spiritual foothold of the Second Coming.

I say "so far", because it is our task as supposedly the very most conscious and watchful branch of humanity, to take up and implement the next stage of the Second Coming: culminating the 21st century with the world's first Threefold Republic, the first outer/external foothold of the Second Coming.

The Twelve Steps are dramatic and visible. But in another sense, they are invisible. You won't see a bearded man with sandals patting Twelve Steppers on the back. But some anthroposophists I've met would not only argue for an invisible Second Coming, but would argue that the Second Coming should have no discernable effect whatsover –that it can and should only be seen by "initiates" and "masters." No. Go to an Open Meeting of AA or NA or Al-Anon or OA...it's just down the block from where you live. There you will see a dramatic and visible Second Coming.

*"**Great changes will take place** during this period [1930 to 1940] and **biblical prophecies will be fulfilled."***

—Rudolf St., "The Reappearance of Christ in the Etheric", Lecture 1

A striking parallelism of events:

Rudolf Steiner affirms that the Second Coming is as dramatic and storied as the biblical events surrounding the Mystery of Golgotha:

*"If you are attentive, you will experience this event of Damascus through direct spiritual observation, and with it clarity and truth about the Christ event. **A striking parallelism of events will take place** ..."*

—"The Reappearance of Christ in the Etheric", Lecture 5.
(The word 'human beings' is replaced with 'you', to help us not wriggle out of it.)

My provisional sussing out of the story suggests that Bill W is playing a role similar to either Zoroaster (the Kingly Jesus) or Paul. Whether Bill bears a more Zoroastrian quality or a Pauline quality remains a question.

Similarly, Dr. Bob is playing a role similar to Peter. Dr. Bob is known in AA circles as "The Rock" and "The Prince of the Twelve Steps". In Bob's eulogy, Bill spoke of him as *"the rock upon which AA was founded."*

These words from Paul ring out especially poignantly if viewed as preparatory prayer for his inauguration of the Second Coming:

*"Feel yourself united in prayer with all other bearers of the spirit—also with me, Paul, so that the power of the word will be given to me **when I am to courageously bring the knowledge of that holy mystery which lives in the message of the gospel.**"*

—Saint Paul's Letter to the Ephesians

To continue the Pauline parallels, Bill's wife, Lois, who co-founded Al-Anon Family Groups, plays a role reminiscent of Silas, with whom Paul was imprisoned.

Lois W (Lois' image was released after her death.)

As for the identity of Zoroaster, or the Bodhisattva, I question the discernment of Anthroposophy if a man who wrote one aesthetic book about ancient Egyptian divination is thereby held up to be humanity's great Turner toward the Good.

Assignment of the Zoroastrian identity is complicated by second-hand reports that Rudolf Steiner stated that Zoroaster was alive in Rudolf Steiner's time as a Bohemian (some say Carpathian) swineherd. . On the one hand, there is no one who proclaimed the more powerfully in the Twentieth Century. If Zoroaster is the Proclaimer of the Etheric Christ (and the

Bodhisattva, World Teacher, and Turner toward the Good) there is no one in the twentieth century who more powerfully and fruitfully proclaimed the Living Christ., except for maybe the likes of Gandhi and MLK.

In these matters of "true myth-making" (inspired perception), Anthroposophic legendry is not only a help—it can also be an overly "mysterious", irksome hindrance. Is there even one anthroposophist who can name the Twelve Bodhisattvas off the top of their head? If Zoroaster was enfleshed as an Eastern European swineherd in Steiner's time, we may "never" know his or her story—so why even bother telling us even those tidbits? Some might say that such personas influence events from a distance. The closest example in 12 Step history I have found in relation to such a possibility is this story:

"We were resolved to admit nobody to A.A. but that hypothetical class of people we termed 'pure alcoholics.' Except for their guzzling, and the unfortunate results thereof, they could have no other complications. So beggars, tramps, asylum inmates, prisoners, queers, plain crackpots, and fallen women were definitely out. Yes sir, we'd cater only to pure and respectable alcoholics! Any others would surely destroy us. Besides, if we took in those odd ones, what would decent people say about us? We built a fine-mesh fence right around A.A. [...]

"What shall the answer be—yes or no?"At first the elders could look only at the objections. "We deal," they said, "with alcoholics only. Shouldn't we sacrifice this one for the sake of the many?" So went the discussion while the newcomer's fate hung in the balance. Then one of the three spoke in a very different voice. "What we are really afraid of," he said, "is our reputation. We are much more afraid of what people might say than the trouble this strange alcoholic might bring. As we've been talking, five short words have been running through my mind. Something keeps repeating to me, 'What would the Master do?'" Not another word was said. What more indeed could be said?"

—Bill W, Chapter Three, *Twelve Steps and Twelve Traditions*

My working hypothesis is that Bill and Bob are parallels of Paul and Peter. And that the parallel of Master Zoroaster was, at that time, a still unidentified person in east-central Europe, who perhaps had a mysterious moral influence on events. I admit I have not mastered all of the details of the Bodhisattva question, the Pauline question, and the Petrine question. My hope is that sharing this work-in-progress with other spiritual scientists will bring clarity sooner or later.

***

Another pair of candidates are the two Gerasene Demoniacs. They are encountered by Christ on "the other side of the sea", in a "tomb" (the depths of addiction), and, once relieved, Christ charged them to share their story:

"'Return to your house and describe what great things God has done for you.' So he went away, proclaiming throughout the whole city what great things Jesus had done for him."

–Gospel of Luke 8:26

There is a similar statement from Bill:

"The Lord has been so wonderful to me curing me of this terrible disease, that I just want to keep talking about it and telling people."

However, this correlation is not so parallel in the sense that the two Demoniacs are not known to have enormously propagated the First Coming over wide swathes of the earth. Whereas Paul and Peter did. As have Bill and Bob in regard to the Second Coming.

Is it "anthroposophic heresy" to suggest that individuals other than Steiner will initiate things which surpass anthroposophy in some ways? As we all know, according to the anthroposophic legendry, Rudolf Steiner is Saint Thomas Aquinas ("The Angelic Theological Doctor of the Church") and Aristotle ("The Father of Logic"). But Thomas Aquinas is not the only authentic Saint of Humanity. Even such a lofty individual is not the only one who is able to initiate something which is entirely pervaded with the true, beautiful, and good. Other leaders of humanity ("saints") will initiate things which come out of their own unique soul qualities, but which are entirely compatible with, and complementary to, Aquinas' reality-shaping work. In fact, Rudolf Steiner speaks of Peter and Paul as bearing a similar stature as Plato and Aristotle:

*"In connection with Raphael's famous painting, "the School of Athens," the question is often raised as to **whether the central figures represent Plato and Aristotle or Peter and Paul. There are just as good reasons for the one view as for the other.**"*

—Rudolf St., "Inner Impulses of Evolution"

Wouldn't be fitting for Schröer, Steiner, Bill, and Bob to play those four roles which are portrayed as the two central figures of Raphael's School of Athens? (Though Schröer reportedly failed in his task, the other three will have brought forth much fruitage in this past century.)

A book handed to me by a local Christian Community priest seems to offer another fitting parallel, from an even earlier epoch—the legendary foundation of Rome:

*"...in a classical boarding school in Ireland, I ran into **"Romulus et Remus"** and realized that the **twin heroes of pagan Rome had been displaced by "Petrus et Paulus", the twin heroes of Christian Rome—the double R ceding smoothly to the double P...**"*

—*The First Paul*, by John Dominic Crossan

The United States is the Roman Empire of our time...the most materially powerful empire in the history of humanity, which is "taxing" the whole world. It would be fitting for the twin heroes of Rome and Christendom to return and turn the tide. Furthermore, the inclusion of gays and lesbians from the start, and the egalitarian role of women in the Fellowships, would be a fitting amends for the one-sidedness results of Pauline theology and Petrine ecclesiasticism. Would it not be fitting for the mythical R&R to be displaced by saints P&P, and to come again as "not saints" B&B?

***

I don't want anyone to stumble over the details. I offer them as stories which are meaningful to me. You're invited to take what is useful to you, and leave the rest on the shelf. But as spiritual scientists, these kinds of questions need to be, and can be, explored. What do you think?

The Fellowships as Archangeloi:
According to my perception, AA is the Archangelos of the Nazarene Order, which prepared humanity's Jewish People to become the vehicle for understanding and embodying the Christ Event.

"The first demand made of a Nazarene was total abstention from all alcohol [...] Those who obeyed the prescribed rules to the letter were obliged to refrain from consuming anything whatsoever derived from the grape."

—Rudolf St., "Deeper Secrets of Human History in the Light of the Gospel of St. Matthew", Lecture III

"John the Baptist prepared for the Pisces Initiation which the Nazarene had to undergo if the Christ was to descend into him."

—Rudolf St., "Background to the Gospel of St. Mark", Lecure 12

In our time, God sent that same Entity to manifest again as the Archangelos of Alcoholics Anonymous, in order to prepare humanity's Alcoholic People to become the vehicle for understanding (or not understanding) and embodying the Second Event, whereby the Representative of Humanity returns in the clouds—the world of enlivening thoughts (concepts) and will forces. Other noble Archangeloi dropped down to become the other Fellowships. Like most Archangeloi, the

Fellowships were human beings during the Universe of Inspiration, which was the second universe prior to our own Universe of Matter and Energy.

The Second Coming is followed by Other Events:

The Akronian Mysteries need to be recognized and understood, because grasping their import unlocks the perception and willingness to enact other events.

*"It will be of the utmost importance to **recognize and understand this event of Christ's Appearance,** for **it will be followed by other events.**"*

—Rudolf St., GA118

Whether I am a member of any Fellowship or not, of course cannot be a matter for public discussion in this book. But to speak personally, do you think it's merely incidental that my familiarity with the Akronian Mysteries has informed my perception of the Threefold Republic and tenacity theretoward?

I offer that the next big "other event" is the Commencement (a word I prefer over "Culmination") of the Anthroposophic Naissance via the establishment of a country-sized Threefold Republic somewhere on earth. Such an "other event" would be of significance on par with the foundation of the Twelve Step Movement in 1935.

humane way—movement for personal recovery and civilizational renewal
an invitation for 4x12 leaders to arise by clearing a golden path

> Don't you know it's darkest before the dawn?
> And it's this thought keeps us moving on
> If we could heed these early warnings
> The time is now quite early morning.
>
> Some say that humankind won't long endure
> But what makes them so doggone sure?
> I know that you who hear my singing
> Could make those freedom bells go ringing.
>
> —Pete Seeger, "Quite Early Morning"

June 24th, 2016[39]

Having myself explored the depths and heights of North American civilization, in the course of my own personal recovery and renewal, I have, for some time, keenly sensed that Anthroposophy, as it exists, simply won't cut it. And yet...I just as keenly sense that there is no better source on which to base the more rarified stages of personal renewal, and also civilizational renewal in the wider fields such as education, agriculture, and state-formation.

So what is to be done?

***

If I look at the fruits of the past century, the lifework of two figures stand out: Rudolf Steiner and William Griffith Wilson. Bill W is the man who pioneered the Recovery way of life in the mid-1930s. Aldous Huxley described Bill as "the greatest social architect of our century", and *Time* magazine named him, simply, "The Healer." He was the proclaimer of a way for anyone to return from death to life, which did not exist prior to 1935. A friend of the early AAs asserted: *"There was a force in Bill that was all his own. It had never been on this earth before, and if Bill did anything to mar it or block it, it would never exist anywhere again."*

Out of these fruits, I have been crafting a completely new iteration of Anthroposophy. Humane Way is a comprehensive synthesis of the Anthroposophic way of knowing and the Twelve Step way of life. Though I am only one person, I aspire to clear a path which totally supersedes Anthroposophy 1.0. This *Humane Way* aims to absorb or replicate every existing organ of the Anthroposophic Society and Movement.

***

Here's how it works. The "lower stages" of the path consists of familiarizing oneself with the existing Recovery fellowships and their offerings, and taking the steps necessary to turn the will towards one's own perception of Higher Power (God, Spiritual World, Higher Ideal)...especially in regard to the "Big Five Wounds" of humanity (chemical substances, co-affliction, eating, sexuality, and soul health). A vast swath of human beings, with representatives in nearly every hamlet and neighborhood in the U.S., are striving day and night along this path, to recover from just one of these wounds.

The "middle stages" of the path consist of immersing oneself in Humanosophic (a.k.a. Anthroposophic)[40] content, such as the Five Basic Texts, the 354 volumes of Total Output (and the 123 issues of further Contributions), the 52 Verses, the Six

---

[39] This text is based on an outline (then called "OnWord Way") which was presented at a Think OutWord core group meeting in Philmont, N.Y. on September 15th, 2013, and again at the "Social/Anti-Social Forces" get-together in Spring Valley on April 27th, 2014. On July 6th, 2014, I began traversing the path myself. Since then, the 4x12 principles have been continually honed via experience. I have journaled about these adventures in a private, anonymized Humane Way blog: https://sites.google.com/site/twelverecoveries/blog/onwordway. Most recently, a sketch of Humane Way was presented at Windy Hill in Harlemville, N.Y. during the community conversations of late 2015 and early 2016.

[40] There is no better way to affirm this "new wine" which cannot be put into an "old wineskin", than to bring forth a new name. Humane Way even aims to re-publish anthroposophic lectures with the words "humane wisdom" and "humanosophic" replacing "anthroposophy" and
(The footnote continues on the next page.)

Essential Exercises, the Eight Exercises for the Days of the Week, the Twelve Virtues, and the 38 Class Lessons. From there the path traverses through the cultural fields of Art, Science, and Religion (or other Worldview).

The "upper stages" of the path consist of economic and social recovery—forming replicable prototypes of civilizational renewal...the outward Kingdom.

The three stages are outlined in one pioneer's own words:

"The path that leads into Humane Way consists
     firstly, then, in **changing the direction of one's will**; [Personal Recovery]
     secondly, in **experiencing supersensible knowledge**; [Humane Wisdom]
     lastly, in **participating in the destiny of one's time** to a point where it becomes one's personal destiny. [Threefold Republic]
One feels oneself sharing humanity's evolution
     in the act of **reversing one's will** [Personal Recovery]
     and **experiencing the supersensible nature of all truth.** [Humane Wisdom]
     Sharing the **experience of the time's true significance** is what gives us our first real feeling for the fact of our humanness. [Threefold Republic]
The term "Humane Way" should really be understood as synonymous with "Sophia," meaning the content of consciousness, the soul attitude and experience that make a person a full-fledged human being. ... In other words,
     the **reversing of the will**, [Personal Recovery]
     the **experiencing of knowledge**, [Humane Wisdom]
     and one's **participation in the time's destiny**, [Threefold Republic]
should all aim at giving the soul a certain direction of consciousness, a 'Sophia.'"
          —Dr. S, Awakening to Community, Lecture 4.
          The word "anthroposophy" is here replaced with "Humane Way."

Personal Recovery is the focus of the first five Quests. Humane Wisdom-based personal and cultural renewal is the focus of the Sixth, Seventh, Eighth, and Ninth Quest. Social renewal via the Threefold Republic is the focus of the Tenth, Eleventh, and Twelfth Quest.

The Twelve Step pathway of Personal Recovery is the chief *personal* manifestation of the Second Coming. Anthroposophy brings the first clear *foresight* and *understanding* of the Second Coming, and will continue to play a role in opening humanity's perception, so that, through our actions, we might consciously contribute to the Beautiful Shepherd's further unfolding in earth. And the Threefold Republic will be the chief *societal* manifestation of the Second Coming.

Humane Way is devoted to embodying the essence of all three.

The Two Predecessor Streams of Humane Way
Humane Way has two parents or predecessors:

▼   The Father Stream: The 12 Step Recovery Movement
▼   The Mother Stream: The Spiritual Scientific Anthroposophic Movement

Humane Way is the Daughter Stream.

Here is one passage from AA which characterizes its foundation in the Father God:

"My friend promised when these things were done I would enter upon a new relationship with my Creator; that I would have the elements of a way of living which answered all my problems. Belief in the power of God, plus enough willingness,

---

"anthroposophic"—similar to how some early Theosophical-era lectures by Dr. S have been re-published with the word "Anthroposophy" instead of "Theosophy."

honesty and humility to establish and maintain the new order of things, were the essential requirements. Simple, but not easy; a price had to be paid. It meant destruction of self-centeredness. I must turn in all things to the **Father of Light** *who presides over us all.*

"These were revolutionary and drastic proposals, but the moment I fully accepted them, the effect was electric. There was a sense of victory, followed by such a peace and serenity as I had never known. There was utter confidence. I felt lifted up, as though the great clean wind of a mountain top blew through and through. God comes to most men gradually, but His impact on me was sudden and profound."

—"Bill's Story", *Alcoholics Anonymous* (the Big Book)
It may be noted that the term "Father of Light" is a Manichæan designation.

By her very name, Anthropo-Sophia reveals her feminine quality. The "motherly" quality of the Anthroposophic Society is expressed here:

"For working in such institutions are also, and in fact mostly, members of the Anthroposophical Society. Now the question is: are these members of the Anthroposophical Society, who work in such a field that has arisen in connection with the Society, despite being the most excellent people in this field, also **always mindful of the mother in the right way**? *Do they from their field work back upon the Anthroposophical Society in the right way?"*

—Dr. S, "Awakening to Community", Lecture 1

...and here, in regard to the Threefold Republic:

"Mother love must be there in the thoughts developed about the social structure *if these thoughts are to have reality in them and not unreality.* **The only form of thought in human life that could be right socially is what is thought out socially with mother love.***"*

—Dr. S, GA 188

That's not to say that the Fellowships don't have a motherly quality, or that the Society doesn't have a fatherly quality, yet this is a meaningful imagination of Humane Way's relationship to the two streams from which she is born.

But the daughter is not co-dependently attached to the limitations of the 12 Step Fellowships-as-they-exist, or to the controloholic or spacey wounds in her mother. We are lovingly detached.

Humane Way aims, through serving as an example, to work back on the Anthroposophical Society, and on the Recovery Movement, in the right way. One parent leans toward arrogance, and the other leans toward self-abasement. Their marriage would magnify the genuine, upright humility of both. Humane Way is an anthroposophically-enhanced Twelve Step Fellowship and a Twelve-Step enhanced Anthroposophic Society.

Dr. S, Bill W, and Dr. Bob (Bill's and Bob's photos were released after their death.)

Five reasons for an engagement between the Twelve Steps and Anthroposophy:

Some might ask: *Why marry the 12 Step Movement?*

Reason #1: Anthroposophia + the 12 Step Movement = a Good Match.

The Twelve Step Movement is complementary with Anthroposophia, and not only in a superficial way. The Fellowships tread where Anthroposophia would not go. The Fellowships are fully in the mainstream of North American life, and yet are authentically devoted to the Representative of Humanity. That the personal renewal which is offered by the Twelve Step rooms is, in a certain sense, beyond or deeper (though more singular) than the mission of anthroposophy is evidenced by this story (forgive me if I don't tell it exactly right, I forget the source): One time, Dr. S was walking with a friend, and they passed by a derelict drunk. The drunk asked Dr. S for help, and he quietly gave him a little money. The friend asked Dr. S why he didn't say some great spiritual wisdom which would help the man. Dr. S replied with sorrow, that a person in that state is beyond the help of anthroposophy.

AA hadn't dropped down yet.

Alcoholic derelicts are not beyond the aid of Alcoholics Anonymous! And so obviously, in this sphere (and similarly "underworldly" afflictions) AA and the other Twelve Step Fellowships bear capacities beyond that of Anthroposophy. On the other hand, AA and the other Fellowships have nothing to say about education (though there are a few Recovery Schools for addicted high schoolers), agriculture, the arts (though there is an Artists in Recovery 12 Step fellowship), and statecraft.

Like Anthroposophia, the Fellowships also speak ancient wisdom, yet through ordinary language.

To give just a few of many examples:

▼ Anthroposophia says that human beings couldn't experience Anger before the Luciferian influence in the Mesozoic Age, and that human beings couldn't experience Fear before the Mephisthophelean influence in the Cenozoic Age. Similarly, the Twelve Step literature characterizes the two "Bogeys" of Pride and Fear.

*"When A.A. suggests a fearless moral inventory, it must seem to every newcomer that more is being asked of him than he can do. **Both his pride and his fear beat him back** every time he tries to look within himself. **Pride says, "You need not pass this way,"** and Fear says, "You dare not look!" But the testimony of A.A.'s who have really tried a moral inventory is that **pride and fear** of this sort **turn out to be bogeymen**, nothing else. Once we have a complete*

willingness to take inventory, and exert ourselves to do the job thoroughly, a wonderful light falls upon this foggy scene."

—Bill W, Chapter Four *Twelve Steps and Twelve Traditions*

▼ The emotional-moral inventory of Steps Four and Eight includes four categories: Resentments, Fears, Sex Conduct, and Harms. These are very concretely equivalent to Anthroposophia's perception of Lucifer, Mephistopheles, the Asuras, and Sorath.

▼ In his writings, Bill W constantly portrays the two extremes, and the health-bringing, uncompromised synthesis. This synthetic thinking has been largely transmitted to the Fellowships as a whole.

Anthroposophia is a good match for the Fellowships because she offers the threefold perspective on everything: the human soul forces (thinking, feeling, willing), the human physical organism (nerve-sense, rhythmic-circulatory, metabolism-limb), the plant (root, leave, flower), the continents (the Americas, Europe-Africa, Asia-Oceania), the higher worlds (the soul world, the lower spiritland, and the upper spiritland), and much else. And what Threefold Recovery is to a human being, so will the Threefold Republic be to a human society.

Humane Way is not just an "anthroposophically-flavored recovery group" in the way that the LDS 12 Step Program is an annex of the Mormon Church. Though Humane Way is anthroposophically enhanced, it's more than that. The 21st century calls for more. The Twelve Steps bear more potential than even AA realizes. And Anthroposophy is tired. The daughter movements are more or less flourishing, but "general anthroposophy" and the Society are a dead horse. And so, Humane Way takes every bit of the substance of Anthroposophy and recasts it into a new shape, using the Three Legacies of AA as the engine. Unlike in Anthroposophy-as-it-exists, the Threefold Republic goal is baked into Humane Way from the start.

Reason #2: We would lengthen the Twelve Steppers' roadway:

The Fellowships sticks out their* hand to human beings who are mired in the swamp. These Archangels place and secure twelve footholds in the mud, so that we might climb out. Once we've climbed out, they points us in the direction of the lights of our home city...the Road of Happy Destiny.

*(Archangeloi don't have a physical gender.)

Humane Way would, in co-operation with the rescue efforts of the Fellowships, serve as a pathfinder past eleven other pitfalls. Humane Way would walk by our side on the long journey home, out of the swamp, up the hill, to the city.

And what the Fellowships are to personal recovery, Humane Way would extend to societal recovery. We strive to bring the Recovery principles and way of life into all spheres of social life—economic, political, and cultural; and at all scales—personal, organizational, local, national, and global. The AA founders cared about what happened to the rest of the world:

*"It occurred to us that we could take what we had into the factories and cause laborers and capitalists to love each other. Our uncompromising honesty might soon clean up politics. With one arm around the shoulder of religion and the other around the shoulder of medicine, we'd resolve their differences. Having learned to live so happily, we'd show everybody else how. Why, we thought, our Society of Alcoholics Anonymous might prove to be **the spearhead of a new spiritual advance! We might transform the world**."*

"Yes, we of A.A. did dream those dreams."

—Bill W. "Tradition Six", *The 12 & 12,* 1953

The Fellowships have cleared a space in the mainstream of life, and are poised to bring a God-grounded, free-thinking, personal renewal to all of humanity. Yet I feel that the Fellowships have a vulnerability. Unless the Recovery principles and way of life penetrate societal structures, including business and government, then I am concerned that the Fellowships, and recovery fellowmen as individuals, may become boxed in.

A little-known secret is that men and women's moral and emotional fiber are frayed by participating in societal harms. It strains one's personal integrity to consciously or unconsciously go along with harm that is enacted by organizations of which I am a member, or to stand by. And a National State is, from the perspective of the spiritual world, simply a large human organization. Continuous, subtly self-inflicted wounds to psychic/soul integrity are not the stuff that advanced sobriety is made of.

"But even suppose blood shed when the conscience is wounded? Through this wound a man's real manhood and immortality flow out, and he bleeds to an everlasting death."

—Thoreau, *Resistance to Civil Government,* 1849

If the 12 Step Fellowships had been present in the Radical Socialist States, or in the National Socialist State, what would recovery have looked like? What would recovery look like in a National Security State?

Unless further avenues of recovery are opened up, some of our fellowmen may heroically escape the fire of addiction, only to be crushed by other afflictions, including seemingly external, societal malaises. I don't want to see anyone awakened, only to find themselves in front of a seemingly unscalable cliff wall. I don't want to see any longtimers live a life of hearty service, only to fall to despair in the end.

There is no question that an afflicted person is useless without abstinence, sobriety, and personal recovery. First things first. And there's no question that we must honor the singleness of purpose of each Fellowship, and avoid outside issues, dissention, and distraction within the Rooms. Yet what potential lies hidden in plain sight within Step Twelve? What might practicing these principles in *all our affairs* look like?

"Possibly, if the AA spent less time and energy in the breadth dimension of spreading AA and more in the length and depth dimension, the breadth of its spread might not be limited to such a low percentage of the world's alcoholics. **The length dimension means the application of the Steps to** **all our affairs***—sedatives, tensions, compulsions, and so on. The depth dimension is suggested by the Eleventh Step, "sought through meditation...for knowledge of His will for us and the power to carry that out."*

—The last message of Ed Dowling, a Jesuit priest, and a Friend of AA, from *The Grapevine* magazine, 1960

Reason #3: The Steps and Traditions would enhance anthroposophy's integrity and harmony:

Maybe it goes without saying, but there is room for improvement in the character of most anthroposophists (including myself).

What does it mean to be an anthroposophist? Maybe nothing. Someone is interested in Rudolf Steiner's lifework. So what? Does that mean the person has embarked on changing their character? Because anthroposophy overs no concrete, accessible path of emotional and volitional healing, we are vulnerable to lingering wounds of flakiness, staleness, and crankiness—or its counterpart: hip anthroposophy which tries to cater to the beau monde of upper class Waldorf customers.

In contrast the Twelve Steps are action-based. Sure, there are people who float in the Rooms without doing the Steps, but at least the actions are obviously central.

Humane Way is, or would be, an action-packed recapitulation of anthroposophy. The foundations of anthroposophy are re-presented as a path of 180 actions.

As for the 12 Traditions: I mean no disrespect to Dr. S, but as organizational principles, the 12 Traditions really outshine anthroposophy's 15 Statutes. I mean, even aesthetically, the Traditions are a polished piece of prose. And they actually work. Lots of people study them for their own sake. Why would people study the dry, dusty 15 Statutes?

The Traditions clarify the relationship to professionalism. In anthroposophy, there is a pervasive but unspoken tendency to view the Waldorf teachers and other anthroposophic professionals as "better than" the ordinary, run-of-the-mill study group attendee; or at least that they are are a different species who seldom mix. The silent influence of the professionalist mindset shapes the conversational quality of Anthroposophic groups via a subtle form of self-censorship. Even years ago, when my work was just barely beginning to unfold, an anthroposophist expressed to me his concern that my revolutionary/evolutionary concepts and efforts for the Threefold Idea would damage the reputation of the professional anthroposophic institutions and organizations. This would be like someone in the Fellowships expressing concern that a member's vigorous quest for personal recovery might affect the reputation of outside 12-step based treatment centers! I was like: mind your own business.

But in Humane Way, it becomes clear that the Home Groups are the only components of Humane Way. Outside institutions—even Humane Way-inspired initiatives and enterprises—have no role in the Fellowship of Humane Way.

Reason #4: A step-based model unpacks and lays out the anthroposophic toolbox:

Reshaping Anthroposophy into a step-based model helps unpack the content, and make it digestable. I have experienced how, even though the source texts have been available for 99 years, hardly any anthroposophist has concretely grasped the details and import of a Threefold Republic, because the details are so scattered and obliquely worded. I've experienced this in regard to other anthroposophic topics as well. Anthroposophy is often undigested...pervasively undigested. And it's not just "our own fault"—though compiled into discrete volumes of Total Output (GA), the anthroposophic offerings are still a big jumbled lump. Humane Way aims to unpack and untangle the content.

Such a twelvefold model also affirms that no particular field of anthroposophy is the "center." I've heard people say that one has to choose between the Society or the Christian Community, or that all anyone needs is eurythmy, or that Waldorf education is of such central importance that it would be better off if it totally disassociated itself from anthroposophy's weird esoteric content, or that anthroposophic art is the most central field since it's the "middle space" between religion and science, or that anthroposophic businessmen are the true Templars and thus the best representatives of anthroposophy. But in Humane Way, each Wayfarer passes through twelve fields of anthroposophic endeavor. The sequential adventures build courage.

Reason #6: A path which really leads to the Threefold Republic is a path to the Upper Spiritland:
In this age, the Upper Spiritland can only be reached through earthly actions. A path which leads from Personal Recovery, through Humane Wisdom, and onward to the Threefold Republic is a path of dying while alive.

*"In a time that comprises about a third of the past earthly life, the soul discovers in spiritual experiences the effect which **this life must have** in accordance with an **ethically just World-order.** During this experience the purpose is begotten in the soul to **shape the next earthly life in a corresponding way**, and thus to compensate for the past."*

—Dr. S, GA 26

Reason #7: By entering into the field of recovery, Anthroposophy will spread and overcome all obstacles:

Dr. S speaks of the necessity of Anthroposophy stepping into even the deepest spheres of affliction:

"Temperance or Moderation [=Recovery] is the virtue which enables humanity to avoid these extremes. Temperance implies neither asceticism nor gluttony, but the happy mean between these two; and this is the virtue of the Spiritual-Soul [the Concioussness Soul, or Soul of Conscious Contact]. Regarding this virtue we have not yet progressed beyond the instinctive standpoint. A little reflection will teach you that, on the whole, people are very much given to sampling the two extremes. They swing to and fro between them. Leaving out of account the few who at the present day endeavour to gain clear views on this subject, you will find that the majority of people live very much after a particular pattern. [...] People themselves ensure that there is excess on one side, and then they get the physicians to prescribe a so-called supressive system of cure, that is, the other extreme, in order that the ill effects may be repaired.

*"From this, it will be seen that in this respect people are still in an instinctive condition, that there is still an instinctive feeling, which is a kind of divine gift, not to go too far in one direction or another. But just as the other instinctive qualities of humanity were lost, **these, too, will be lost** [...]This quality which is still possessed as a natural tendency **will be lost**; and now you will be able to judge how much the world conception and conviction of anthroposophy will have to contribute in order gradually to develop consciousness in this field.*

*"At the present time **there are very few, even developed Anthroposophists,** who see clearly that **anthroposophy provides the means to gain the right consciousness in this field also."***

And what will be the result? Dr. S continues...

*"**When anthroposophy is able to bring more weight to bear in this direction,** then will appear what I can only describe in the following way; people will gradually **long more and more for great spiritual truths.***

*"Although Anthroposophy is still scorned today, it will not always be so. **It will spread, and overcome all its external opponents and everything else still opposing it**"*

—Dr. S, "The Spiritual Foundation of Morality"

If and when Anthroposophia deigns to dirty her hands and open up new avenues of recovery, then human beings of all stripes will become genuinely interested in Anthroposophia. In that way, she will spread and overcome all external obstacles and hindrances.

Humane Way brings more weight to bear in this direction.

The Four Legacies of Humane Way

Humane Way is a path composed of 4x12 principles, known as the Four Legacies. The Four Legacies are the existing Three Legacies authored by Bill W, plus a Fourth Legacy through which these principles are applied to all of life.

- ▼ The Twelve Steps for Personal Recovery

- ▼ The Twelve Traditions for Group Singularity (AA's "Group Unity")

- ▼ The Twelve Concepts for Organismic Service (AA's "World Service")

- ▼ The Twelve Quests for Civilizational Renewal

Here is a provisional draft of the Four Legacies, as adapted for Humane Way. The Twelve Steps and Twelve Quests are temporarily worded as "I", because at this point in the story (June 2016), only one human being has enacted the Steps in the context of Humane Way. When another person has stepped up this twelvefold pathway, the text will be changed to "we", and the wording will be honed to reflect their experience as well. The wording of the Twelve Traditions, and even moreso the Twelve Concepts, are in flux until a World Service Body of Humane Way is formed and affirms a final text for publication.

***

The First Legacy:
Twelve Steps for Personal Recovery

*"If we seek to penetrate the mysteries of human nature through our own efforts, we must abide by the golden rule of the occult sciences. This rule states: '**For every single step** that you take in seeking knowledge of hidden truths, you must **take three steps** in perfecting your character toward the good.'"*

—Dr. S, How to Know Higher Worlds

"Many people, nonalcoholics, report that as a result of the practice of A.A.'s Twelve Steps, they have been able to meet other difficulties of life. They think that the Twelve Steps can mean more than sobriety for problem drinkers. They see in them a way to happy and effective living for many, alcoholic or not."

—Bill W, foreword to The Twelve Steps and Twelve Traditions

▼ **Step One:** *I admitted my unenhanced human willpower was less powerful than an inner or outer affliction or hindrance—that my life was in distress.*

▼ **Step Two:** *I came to conceive that a Power beyond my ordinary self could restore me to sanity, health, and freedom.*

▼ **Step Three:** *I made a decision to turn my will and whole life over to the care and service of a loving God or Ideal of my own perception. I resolved to traverse all twelve Steps.*

▼ **Step Four:** *I wrote a thorough emotional and moral inventory of myself, including a list of resentments, fears, and sexual conduct. For each hurt I'd received in life, I named at least one action or character quality of my own which played a role.*

▼ **Step Five:** *I admitted to my Higher Power, to myself, and to another human being exactly what harms I did, or considered doing. I opened up my most shameful episodes to the light of a higher witness and a human witness.*

▼ **Step Six:** *I prepared to be guided to my Higher Power toward resolution of all of these character flaws, so that from the foundation of enacting these Steps, all my missteps, ugly actions, and harm-doing will eventually be transformed.*

▼ **Step Seven:** *I humbly asked my Higher Power to bring all of my shortcomings to closure and completion. I resolved to trudge onward to the summit of making personal amends.*

▼ **Step Eight:** *I wrote a list of all persons, groups, and beings I have ever harmed in my entire life, and resolved to make restitution to each of them.*

▼ **Step Nine:** *I went and apologized, offering concrete or symbolic restitution to each of these people. I held back only when my approach would do more harm to them than good.*

▼ **Step Ten:** *I continue to maintain a daily or periodic personal inventory, so that when I make a mistake, I promptly admit it.*

▼ **Step Eleven:** *I seek through prayer, spiritual study, and meditation to hone my conscious, soulful communication with the Higher Power of my own perception, seeking foremost for knowledge of Higher Power's goals for myself and humanity, and the power to implement that.*

▼ **Step Twelve:** *Having experienced a threefold metamorphosis—a change in thoughts, feelings, and actions—as a result of traversing these steps, I bear a loving responsibility to carry this message to those human beings who still suffer, and to extend these twelve principles into all fields of life.*

***

The Second Legacy:
Twelve Traditions for Group Singularity

"There is, too, a rising interest in the Twelve Traditions of Alcoholics Anonymous. Students of human relations are beginning to wonder how and why A.A. functions as a society. Why is it, they ask, that in A.A. no member can be set in personal authority over another, that nothing like a central government can anywhere be seen? How can a set of traditional principles, having no legal force at all, hold the Fellowship of Alcoholics Anonymous in unity and effectiveness? The second section of this volume, though designed for A.A.'s membership, will give such inquirers an inside view of A.A. never before possible."

—Bill W, foreword to *The Twelve Steps and Twelve Traditions*

▼ **Tradition One:** *Unity is not uniformity—we respect the sacred fact that each human being bears their own individual conscience. And so we practice the "Law of Mobility": to start a new Humane Way group, all it takes is a grudge and two feet. If at any time during our path together we find ourselves in any situation where we are neither learning nor* *contributing, we are welcome to use our two feet, and venture forth on our own individual way. Each individual is free to pioneer a new group, to revise and adapt the Humane Way principles and texts, and even to form an allied offshoot, with its own name. And yet our common wellbeing comes first; personal progress for the greatest number depends upon unity-in-diversity, that is, true singularity. Yet the fulfillment of individual needs and capacities follows soon after. Some iteration of Humane Way must continue to flourish, or most of us will eventually fall by the wayside.*

▼ **Tradition Two:** *For the purpose of our groups and their service organisms, there is but one legitimate authority—a loving God or Ideal as may be expressed in our collective conscience. Our leaders are but trusted servants—they do not govern. We value leadership and initiative, but we have no governors.*

▼ **Tradition Three:** *We would be happy for all human beings to join Humane Way. We may refuse none who wish to traverse this path of recovery and renewal. Hence, the only requirement for membership in Humane Way is an interest in some aspect of the Four Legacies. Membership must never be tied to money or conformity. Secular minds and believers are equally welcome. A person is a member if they say or feel they are. All members are co-founders of the continually unfolding Humane Way impulse. Any two or three human beings gathered together to practice the Four Legacies are welcome to call themselves a Humane Way group. As long as the Four Legacies are central, such a group may very well study or practice principles from other streams of culture, thereby marrying our principles with any and all existing wisdom traditions.*

▼ **Tradition Four:** *Each group is an independent and self-governing fellowship, society, collectivity, and micro-republic. Each group is free to author its own local literature, to revise and reprint texts published by other Humane Way service organisms, and even to adapt the wording of the Four Legacies to reflect its singular local mission. Yet we consult with each other in matters which might greatly affect another group or Humane Way as a whole. To change the wording of the Four Legacies within the publications of the World Service Organism, requires approval from ¾ of world-confederated groups.*

▼ **Tradition Five:** *Each group is a spiritual entity which bears one singular purpose—to carry its message to those human beings who still suffer. We do this by practicing the Four Legacies of Humane Way ourselves.*

▼ **Tradition Six:** *A Humane Way group never endorses, finances, or affiliates with any non-Humane Way endeavor, lest problems of money, property, and prestige divert us from our singular purpose. However, the Twelve Step fellowships and Anthroposophic organizations are considered to be "farm teams" of Humane Way, and we actively commend Wayfarers to their spiritual tutelage. Likewise, any and all Twelve Step literature and Anthroposophic literature is affirmed as relevant to Humane Way study and practice. The Humane Way name is not trademarked, and thus cannot be lent or licensed out. However, given the comprehensive scope of our pathway, there is no limit to the creation of Humane Way-inspired facilities—clubhouses, service centers, schools and colleges, clinics, farms, intentional communities, and other enterprises—which apply the Four Legacies to their field of activity. However, when a Humane Way initiative involves significant property, assets, or administration it is separately incorporated, thus differentiating the general spiritual purpose of the Humane Way groups, as such, from specialized cultural, social, and economic bodies inspired by Humane Way principles. Humane Way groups are generally places for the study and practice of the Four Legacies at a local, sociable, humble scale which can be readily pioneered by any Wayfarer. Though for the practical purpose of carrying our message, we may temporarily collaborate with any outside entity, such co-working should never lead to affiliation or endorsement, formal or implied. A Humane Way group bows and binds itself to no one but its loving collective conscience.*

▼ **Tradition Seven:** *Every group becomes fully self-supporting through the voluntary gifting of its own members. Though established groups are welcome to temporarily support fledgling groups, our groups and service organisms accept no money or gifts from anyone who is not a member of Humane Way. He who pays the piper is apt to call the tune. We view the acceptance of large monies from a single Humane Way member, or tied to any actual or implied obligation, as folly. So too for Humane Way treasuries which accumulate beyond a prudent reserve, for no known purpose. Our predecessors warn that nothing can so destroy our spiritual substance as hopeless bickering over monied power.*

▼ **Tradition Eight:** *Within the groups and their service organisms, our usual Humane Way twelfth step work remains forever non-professional, non-commercial, and non-monetized, but our service centers may employ or contract* specialized co-workers for support tasks for which we might otherwise have to hire non-Wayfarers. We define professionalism as the job of teaching or counseling the Four Legacies for pay. However, outside of the groups, Humane Way-inspired enterprises and initiatives could provide services which maintain a staff whose vocation is related to certain aspects of the Four Legacies (such as schoolteacher or farmer working in a Humane Way-inspired school or farm), while keeping in mind the spiritual-cultural principle of "freely ye have received, freely give" and the economic principle of a fair, transparent, "true price" which accounts for the triple bottom line: humanity, the land, and fruitful profit. In Humane Way, professional roles ought never trump human siblinhood and the loving conscience.

▼ **Tradition Nine**: *Our groups are not meant to be bureaucratically organized. We aim for the least amount of organization necessary to be effective. However, our groups may create service bodies, confederated service organisms, and committees thereof, as ad-hoc tools which serve to more widely propagate the message of the groups. Rotation of leadership is the watchword. The sovereign group elects its secretary or rotating committee of trusted servants, as do their confederated service organisms, perhaps with paid office staff. The groups' delegation of responsibility to service organisms is guided by the Twelve Concepts for Service. The 4x12 trustees of the World Service Body are the world-scale equivalent of the group officers. The World Service Organism, and other confederated service organisms, serve as the chief handler of public relations at the level of their mandated scale or theme. At all levels, our leadership derives no outer authority from their titles; personal virtue and experience with enacting the Four Legacies are the spiritual keys to their fruitfulness.*

▼ **Tradition Ten:** *Given the comprehensive mission of Humane Way, we do hold a viewpoint on potentially all economic, political, and cultural issues of concern to humanity. However, our name and voice ought not be unnecessarily and prematurely drawn into public controversy via partisan politics or via allegiance to councils, movements, and states which are not fully imbued with the Four Legacies. We supersede by example, moreso than by opposition. However, there may be moments when we collectively say "No. Enough."*

▼ **Tradition Eleven:** *Our public relations policy is based on serving as an exemplar rather than sensational glamour. We avoid flashy advertising. We are obliged to maintain the effacement of names and visages of living Humane Way members at the level of newspapers, books, magazines, radio, films, television, internet, and social media. Though we favor the principle of attraction rather than promotion, we do, however, actively propagate our anonymized message via any and all transparent means. The fruits of our deeds speak for themselves.*

▼ **Tradition Twelve:** *Self-effacement is the spiritual cornerstone of our Twelve Traditions, ever calling us to place principles above personalities. Within these rooms, we go only by our first name and last initial (or nickname), so that we are aesthetically immersed in a new culture based on personal individuation and action-based virtue, rather than on inherited bloodlines, on money-based hierarchy and celebrity, or on infallible gurudom and sainthood. In Humane Way, we are all pioneers and initiators; but we are not saints. May the beautiful fruits we have gathered by walking this pathway never ruin us, that we may continually dwell near the loving splendor of our individual and collective Higher Powers, and become ever more free and loving Representatives of Humanity.*

***

The Third Legacy:
Twelve Concepts for Organismic Service

▼ **Concept I:** *Singularity—Just as the responsibility and authority for group services belongs to the individual members, so too the ultimate responsibility and authority for Humane Way world services, and for other confederated service organisms, belongs entirely to the Humane Way groups. Each group is an independent, singular entity in its own right, and is the only level of sovereignty in Humane Way besides the sovereignty of the singular human being. A group can retrieve its delegated authority at any time by deregistering the service organism, or by joining with another like-minded group to form a new service organism. The spiritual principles behind these Twelve Concepts are relevant even to groups which do not participate in confederated services, because each group is also a Group Service Organism.*

▼ **Concept II:** *Conscience—In a similar way that group-scale services are maintained through a Group Service Assembly (also known as a Group Business Meeting or Group Conscience Meeting), the Humane Way groups have delegated to* the World Service Assembly the maintenance of our world-scale services; thus, the World Service Assembly is the voice and conscience of Humane Way at a world-wide scale. Other confederated service assemblies maintain and serve as the voice and conscience of other geographic scales or thematic streams.

▼ **Concept III:** *Trust—The right of decision makes effective leadership possible.*

▼ **Concept IV:** *Equality—Participation is the key to harmony.*

▼ **Concept V:** *Consideration—The rights of appeal and petition protect minorities and insure that they be heard.*

▼ **Concept VI:** *Responsibility—The World Service Assembly acknowledges the primary administrative responsibility of the 4x12 Trusted Servants. Other confederated service assemblies designate their own leadership. Responsibility is also responsiveness and 'respond-ability'—the ability and willingness to respond.*

▼ **Concept VII**: *Balance—The World Service Body of 4x12 Trusted Servants has legal rights and responsibilities accorded to them by Humane Way Bylaws; the rights and responsibilities of the World Service Assembly are accorded to it by Custom. Other confederated service bodies and assemblies create their own bylaws and customs.*

▼ **Concept VIII:** *Delegation—The World Service Body has delegated to an Administrative Committee the responsibility to administer their World Service Office, also known as the World Headquarters or World Service Center.*

▼ **Concept IX:** *Virtue—Good personal leadership at all service levels is a necessity. In the field of world service the World Service Body assumes the primary leadership. Other confederated service bodies provide leadership in their own fields.*

▼ **Concept X:** *Clarity—Service responsibility is balanced by carefully defined service authority and double-headed management is avoided.*

▼ **Concept XI:** *Humility—The World Service Center, and other confederal service centers, should always be assisted by the best standing committees, administrators, staffs and consultants.*

▼ **Concept XII:** *Guardianship—The spiritual groundwork for Humane Way service ensures the...*

...Seven Warranties of the Assembly:

Warranty A. *Selflessness—No Humane Way service organism, body, assembly, or committee shall ever become the seat of perilous wealth or power. We guard ourselves from peril in these ways:*

Seven Safety Seats of Warranty A:

▽ **Safety Seat #1.** *Names and Logos—The Humane Way name is composed of two words which are part of the common heritage of humankind—"humane" and "way." Similarly, the triangle, circle, and square diamond are universal shapes. Hence the Humane Way name and logo ought never be copyrighted or trademarked. If outside enterprises encroach upon our symbology to an extent that greatly distracts from our message, Humane Way is deft enough to evolve a fresh moniker and symbol.*

▽ **Safety Seat #2.** *Free Culture—Our Humane Way principles are adapted from freely given spiritual wisdom, distilled from the common cultural heritage of humankind. Humane Way is devoted to an open source culture of "freely ye have received, freely give." Thus Humane Way-authored books ought never be copyrighted. Anyone is free to reprint and adapt our message, whether for non-profit or for profit, and even to place their own name on our text. The message is of more import than the messenger. We welcome those who adapt our message to contact us so that we might keep abreast of these offshoots, but it is not a matter of withholding or granting permission, as we have already released our texts into the domain of free culture. In this way, literature sales and publishing rights will never be a source of perilous wealth or power. From the start, our World Service Organism and other confederated service organisms will operate in a way which correlates with their humble budget and mandate. Creative but non-*

compulsory means will unfold to evoke consciousness of the funding needs of service organisms among the groups.

∇ **Safety Seat #3.** *Geographic Monopolies—No service organism may enforce a geographic monopoly. Humane Way service bodies ought never be conceptually fused with nation-states or their legal-jurisdictional boundaries. Just as there may be a confederate service organism which serves more than one nation-state, it is likewise acceptable for there to be more than one "competing" service organism within a single nation-state. We favor neither lumping or splitting. Each group is essentially a sovereign World Service Organism with regard to its own local message, and while for most practical purposes its service area is localized, there is no actual geographic limitation to the scope or outreach of any group. As cultural spaces, rather than political borders, the geographic service areas of various groups and service organisms are free to overlap with each other. The World Service Organism is the World Fellowship, while each group is a Group Fellowship: Humane Way is a Fellowship of Fellowships, a Society of Societies, an Association of Associations, a Collective of Collectivities, and a Republic of Republics.*

∇ **Safety Seat #4.** *The Group is a World—Legally and spiritually, each Humane Way groups is an independent entity. Confederated service organisms bear no permanent sovereignty, and are formed as confederal, ad-hoc tools to implement the shared will of multiple sovereign groups. And so a service organism can never be punitive or exercise a formative influence on the sovereign groups which it serves. The groups which have temporarily pooled their authority via a service organism can, however, freely decide what criteria a group must meet in order to join or remain a member of the confederated organism, and thereby be listed in their confederated meeting list.*

∇ **Safety Seat #5.** *Multiple, Mutual Registrations—A group is free to belong to multiple confederated service organisms, or to none. The World Service Organism is essentially just another confederated service organism, but whose scope is geographically and thematically comprehensive. Rather than groups deigning to "register" with confederated service offices, the group and the service office mutually register each other, and assign each other a number. Instead of "registered groups", we have "registering groups."*

∇ **Safety Seat #6.** *School Allegiances—At all service levels, the selection of the leadership must never be explicitly or implicitly tied to membership in specific schools or circles. Though Humane Way members are free as individuals to pioneer Four Legacy-inspired esoteric schools or circles, the only "schooling" that counts in Humane Way is the traversing of the Four Legacies.*

∇ **Safety Seat #7:** *Generational Metamorphosis—Humane Way exists to serve the living generation of humanity, and should never become a ghost which lingers and tyrannically shapes the formative forces of the emerging youth. The legal and customary framework of Humane Way exists for only a generation—every 21 years, the Fellowship of Humane Way dissolves into an imago state, and its Four Legacies, Body and bylaws, Assembly and customs, must be completely revised and renewed, emerging afresh from its chrysalis.*

Warranty B. *Realism—Sufficient operating funds, plus an ample reserve, shall be Humane Way's prudent financial principle;*

Warranty C. *Representation—No Humane Way member shall ever be placed in a position of unqualified authority. No Humane Way service organism ought to use titles which transcend the common aesthetic of the sovereign local groups. Thus, group service officers are also referred to as "group trustees", and the world trustees are also known as "world service officers." All are trusted servants. A group business meeting or group conscience meeting is also a Group Service Assembly. If there is no differentiation between a group steering committee (composed of the group's officers) and the general group conscience, then the Group Assembly is also the Group Service Body. Likewise, the Area Service Assembly and World Service Assembly are also referred to as "Area Conscience Meeting" and "World Conscience Meeting" Similarly, the group secretary is also an informal "group executive director", and the world executive director is also "world secretary." In this way we avoid attaching prestige and glamour to the wider, confederated echelons of service hierarchy. We thereby assure that the sovereign Humane Way group is the model for all levels of service.*

Warranty D. *Dialogue—All important decisions shall be reached by discussion, vote and, whenever possible, by substantial unanimity;*

Warranty E. *Compassion—No service action shall ever be personally punitive. There ought to be no reason to sue or be sued in Humane Way. Service-related disagreements are resolved through frank discussion, listening, mediation, personal entreaty, and virtue.*

Warranty F. *Courage—Given the comprehensive mission of Humane Way, there may be moments where we take a public stand before the eye of the world. However, we choose our battles. Our service actions ought to sidestep unnecessary public controversy and circus-like political spectacle. We navigate through or around hopelessly polarized morasses; and*

Warranty G. *Respect—No Humane Way service organism shall ever perform any acts of compulsory government, and each shall always remain humanocratic—in other words: radically decentralized, egalitarian, and participatory—in thought and action.*

***

The Fourth Legacy:
144 Adventures of the Twelve Quests for Civilizational Renewal
(Intense Version)

*"**Everything in the world** develops twelve different aspects or nuances."*

—Dr. S, June 6th, 1906

*"Having had a spiritual awakening as the result of these steps, we tried to carry this message to other addicts, **and to practice these principles in all our affairs.**"*

—Bill W, The Twelve Steps

In Humane Way, we each enact the 12 Steps, we each do a study of the 12 Traditions, and a study of the 12 Concepts. The Fourth Legacy is the Twelve Quests, which are an entirely new development. The Twelve Quests are a distillation and organic recapitulation of the entire content of Anthroposophy.

Each of the Twelve Quests is made of Twelve Adventures, making for 144 Adventures. An Adventure is an autarchic, self-selected action, which could be as simple as visiting a single 12 Step meeting or Anthroposophic study group, or reading a single piece of literature...even an article or pamphlet. Or an adventure could be as intense and elaborate as pioneering a new enterprise or initiative.

The Three Legacies could be enacted before the Twelve Quests, or they could be enacted in conjunction with the Quests. Namely, the Twelve Steps fit naturally in the passage through the Big Five Wounds (the first five Quests). The Twelve Traditions study is related to the Tenth Quest (social renewal). And the Twelve Concepts study is relevant to the Twelfth Quest (civilizational renewal). The 12 Steps, the 12 Traditions study, the 12 Concepts study, and the 144 Adventures makes for 180 actions in all (12+12+12+144 = 180).

The first five Quests are temporarily worded as "I", because as of June 2016 no one else has done these actions yet in the context of Humane Way. The sixth through twelfth Quests are worded as "I aim to" because I myself haven't done them yet. When another person has traversed a semblance of this path, then the wording would be changed to "We."

▼ **The Twelve Adventures of the First Quest—Substance Use and Physical Wellbeing:** *I [We] recovered from alcohol[41], drugs (including cannabis), and nicotine. I [We] became clean and sober through complete and total abstinence. Honoring my [our] physical body as the material foundation for emotional and spiritual progress, I [we] began to address any physical ailments, while becoming aware of holistically enhanced sources of healing and fitness, and mindful that each affliction of humankind holds the potential for a shared transcendence of pain and suffering, as a specific karmic group.*

    ▽ **The First Legacy**: *At some point during my [our] path through the "Big Five Wounds of Humanity", I [we each] enacted the Twelve Steps for Personal Recovery.*

---

[41] Q: *"How much alcohol is a person on a spiritual path permitted to have?"*
Dr. S: *"Not even as much as one chocolate liqueur."*

▼ **The Twelve Adventures of the Second Quest—Co-Affliction and Individuation:** *I [We] practiced recovering from co-affliction—navigating between the poles of people-pleasing and controloholism. In regard to unhealthy dynamics in my [our] circles of family, friends, and associates, I [we] practiced loving detachment, setting boundaries, and individuation. I [We] became my [our] own person.*

▼ **The Twelve Adventures of the Third Quest—Food and Eating:** *I [We] practiced recovering from destructive eating and devitalizing foods. I [We] adopted [either a 'carnosophic' (flesh-wise) or] 'vegesophic' (plant-wise) way of eating—composed of nearly 100% Organic food, and Biodynamic where available. I [We] almost totally abstained from dead sugar, including foodstuffs where cane sugar is one of the first three ingredients. Instead, I [we] allowed myself [ourselves] to enjoy 'living sweetness' such as organic maple syrup and honey. Beyond my [our shared] devotion to Organic and Biodynamic quality, and [shared] abstinence from white sugar, I [we each] developed my [our] own individual food plan.*

▼ **The Twelve Adventures of the Fourth Quest—Sexuality and Relationship:** *I [We] practiced recovery in the fields of harm-free sexuality, partnership, and gender issues.*

▼ **The Twelve Adventures of the Fifth Quest—Emotional and Mental Wellbeing:** I [We] practice recovery from raised and lowered feelings and suicidality. Through soulcare, I [we] reached for emotional sobriety, balance, and serenity.

▼ **The Twelve Adventures of the Sixth Quest—Esoteric Knowledge and Wisdom:** *Having traversed the Twelve Steps, I aim to practice [we practiced] renewal of <u>humanosophy</u> (humane wisdom) through esoteric study and research, prayer and verses, mindfulness and meditation. I aim to seek for [We sought] the <u>Wisdom</u> to navigate between two poles: on the one hand, <u>serene acceptance</u>, and the other hand, <u>the courage to change</u>—that is, the golden mean. Signposts on the humanosophic path include: the Five Basic Texts, the 354 volumes of Total Output and the 123 issues of further Contributions, the 52 Verses, the Six Essential Exercises, the Eight Exercises for the Days of the Week, the Twelve Virtues for the Months of the Year, the 38 Class Lessons, and further waymarkers as may be revealed to each human being, through our own individual gnosis.*

▼ **The Twelve Adventures of the Seventh Quest—Religion and Philosophy:** *I aim to practice [We practiced] renewing my [our] personal worldview—my [our] religion, spiritual tradition, or philosophy—the myriad of potentially humane mysteries. I aim to deepen [We deepened] my [our] feeling life through religious, mystical, or philosophic ceremony and communion. As an individual and as a member of groups [As individuals and groups], I aim to make [we made] amends for the harm done in the name of my worldview [our worldviews].*

▼ **The Twelve Adventures of the Eighth Quest—Sciences and Humanities:** *I aim to practice [We practiced] renewing the sciences and humanities, including art of education. I aim to pioneer my [We pioneered our] own humanosophically-inspired schools and micro-colleges. I aim to make [We made] amends for the harm done by scientism.*

▼ **The Twelve Adventures of the Ninth Quest—Arts and Handwork:** *I aim to practice [We practiced] renewing the fine and practical arts and crafts.*

▼ **The Twelve Adventures of the Tenth Quest—Social Arts and Community:** *I aim to practice [We practiced] social renewal through the conversational arts, through humanizing our political spectrum, through intentional community-building, and through play. I aim to learn [We learned] to tell my [our] left hand from my [our] right hand, discerning the one-sidedness of both privatism (corporatism) and governmentalism (statism). I aim to make [We made] amends for the intentional and unintentional harm done by my [our] political allegiances, my [our] family lineage[s], nation[s], races, and other social groups in which I [we] have found myself [ourselves] enfleshed.*

    ▽ **The Second Legacy:** *I aim to study and apply [We studied and applied] the Twelve Traditions for Group Singularity in my [our] own life [lives] and groups.*

▼ **The Twelve Adventures of the Eleventh Quest—Householding and Economics:** *I aim to practice [We practiced] economic renewal. Through addressing the personal, micro-economic afflictions of my [our] household—such as shoplifting and thievery, compulsive gambling, overshopping and consumerism, clutter and hoarding, demoralizing* *debt, work-shyness versus workaholism, and financial illiteracy—I aim to begin [we began] to develop clarity and effectiveness in regard to transforming macro-economic malaise, unfairness, and exploitation. I aim to make [We made] amends for the harm done by economic bodies we have patronized. I aim to form [We formed] transparent, asssociative economic commonwealths of 50 to 100 households to feed humanity, in service of a sacred, living economy.*

▼ **The Twelve Adventures of the Twelfth Quest—Trisecting and World Repair:** *I aim to practice [We practiced] world renewal...civilizational recovery. I aim to [We] courageously pioneer[ed] a parallel Threefold Republic, even if it be symbolic at first. By becoming spiritual siblings, I aim to recover [we recovered] from <u>war fever</u>. I aim to [We] strive to unfold as-yet-unrealized dimensions:*

...of length, through applying these principles in further and further aspects of life;

...of depth, through ever clearer, more nuanced, conscious communication with our personal and collective Higher Powers;

...and of breadth, through carrying the message of this path to those human beings who still suffer, in each and every nook and cranny of the whole wide world.

∇ **The Third Legacy:** *I aim to study and apply [We studied and applied] the Twelve Concepts for Confederal Service in my [our] own life [lives] and societies.*

***

The Fourth Legacy:
144 Adventures of the Twelve Quests for Civilizational Renewal
(Freeform Version)

Another way to go about the Twelve Quests is simply to enact 144 Adventures in any twelve fields of one's own choosing, with these twelve serving only as an example:

1. **Substance Use[42] and Physical Wellbeing**
2. **Co-Affliction and Individuation**
3. **Food and Eating[42]**
4. **Sexuality and Relationship**
5. **Emotional and Mental Wellbeing**
6. **Esoteric Knowledge and Wisdom**
7. **Religion and Philosophy**
8. **Sciences and Humanities**
9. **Arts and Handwork**
10. **Social Arts and Community**
11. **Householding and Economics**
12. **Trisecting and World Repair**

"Great events will come to pass for you and countless others."

—Bill W, "A Vision for You" from the Big Book of *Alcoholics Anonymous*

---

[42]*"**I never tell anyone whether or not he should abstain** from alcohol, or whether he should eat vegetables instead of meat. Instead I explain how alcohol works. I simply describe how it works; then the person may decide to drink or not as he pleases. I do the same regarding vegetarian or meat diets. I simply say, this is how meat works and this is how plants work. The result is that a person can decide for himself. Above all else, science must have respect for human freedom, so that a person never has the feeling of being given orders or forbidden to do something. He is only told the facts. Once he knows how alcohol works, he will discover on his own what is right. This way we shall accomplish the most. We will come to the point where free human beings can choose their own directions. We must strive for this. Only then will we have real social reforms."* —Dr. S, GA 348

The 180 Actions:
A Personal Tally

The Twelve Steps are typically done sometime between the First and Fifth Recovery, before moving on the Sixth Recovery. The Twelve Traditions study is usually done in the vicinity of the Tenth Recovery, while the Twelve Concepts are associated with the Twelfth Recovery.

The First Recovery (substances/health)
Adventure 1_____
Adventure 2_____
Adventure 3_____
Adventure 4_____
Adventure 5_____
Adventure 6_____
Adventure 7_____
Adventure 8_____
Adventure 9_____
Adventure 10_____
Adventure 11_____
Adventure 12_____

The Second Recovery
(co-affliction/individuation)
Adventure 13_____
Adventure 14_____
Adventure 15_____
Adventure 16_____
Adventure 17_____
Adventure 18_____
Adventure 19_____
Adventure 20_____
Adventure 21_____
Adventure 22_____
Adventure 23_____
Adventure 24_____

The Third Recovery (food/eating)
Adventure 25_____
Adventure 26_____
Adventure 27_____
Adventure 28_____
Adventure 29_____
Adventure 30_____
Adventure 31_____
Adventure 32_____
Adventure 33_____
Adventure 34_____
Adventure 35_____
Adventure 36_____

The Fourth Recovery (sexuality/relationship)
Adventure 37_____
Adventure 38_____
Adventure 39_____
Adventure 40_____
Adventure 41_____
Adventure 42_____
Adventure 43_____
Adventure 44_____
Adventure 45_____
Adventure 46_____
Adventure 47_____
Adventure 48_____

The Fifth Recovery (emotional/mental)
Adventure 49_____
Adventure 50_____
Adventure 51_____
Adventure 52_____
Adventure 53_____
Adventure 54_____
Adventure 55_____

Adventure 56_____
Adventure 57_____
Adventure 58_____
Adventure 59_____
Adventure 60_____

The Twelve Steps
(personal recovery)
Step One_____
Step Two_____
Step Three_____
Step Four_____
Step Five_____
Step Six_____
Step Seven_____
Step Eight_____
Step Nine_____
Step Ten_____
Step Eleven_____
Step Twelve_____

The Sixth Recovery
(humane wisdom)
Adventure 61_____
Adventure 62_____
Adventure 63_____
Adventure 64_____
Adventure 65_____
Adventure 66_____
Adventure 67_____
Adventure 68_____
Adventure 69_____
Adventure 70_____
Adventure 71_____
Adventure 72_____

The Seventh Recovery
(religion/philosophy/worldview)
Adventure 73_____
Adventure 74_____
Adventure 75_____
Adventure 76_____
Adventure 77_____
Adventure 78_____
Adventure 79_____
Adventure 80_____
Adventure 81_____
Adventure 82_____
Adventure 83_____
Adventure 84_____

The Eighth Recovery (science/humanities)
Adventure 85_____
Adventure 86_____
Adventure 87_____
Adventure 88_____
Adventure 89_____
Adventure 90_____
Adventure 91_____
Adventure 92_____
Adventure 93_____
Adventure 94_____
Adventure 95_____
Adventure 96_____

The Ninth Recovery (art/handwork)
Adventure 97_____
Adventure 98_____
Adventure 99_____
Adventure 100_____
Adventure 101_____
Adventure 102_____
Adventure 103_____
Adventure 104_____
Adventure 105_____
Adventure 106_____
Adventure 107_____
Adventure 108_____

The Tenth Recovery (social/community)
Adventure 109_____
Adventure 110_____
Adventure 111_____
Adventure 112_____
Adventure 113_____
Adventure 114_____
Adventure 115_____
Adventure 116_____
Adventure 117_____
Adventure 118_____
Adventure 119_____
Adventure 120_____

The Twelve Traditions
(group singularity)
Tradition One_____
Tradition Two_____
Tradition Three_____
Tradition Four_____
Tradition Five_____
Tradition Six_____
Tradition Seven_____
Tradition Eight_____
Tradition Nine_____
Tradition Ten_____
Tradition Eleven_____
Tradition Twelve_____

The Eleventh Recovery
(householding/economic)
Adventure 121_____
Adventure 122_____
Adventure 123_____
Adventure 124_____
Adventure 125_____
Adventure 126_____
Adventure 127_____
Adventure 128_____
Adventure 129_____
Adventure 130_____
Adventure 131_____
Adventure 132_____

The Twelfth Recovery
(threefold republic)
Adventure 133_____
Adventure 134_____
Adventure 135_____
Adventure 136_____
Adventure 137_____
Adventure 138_____
Adventure 139_____
Adventure 140_____
Adventure 141_____
Adventure 142_____
Adventure 143_____
Adventure 144_____

The Twelve Concepts
(organismic service)
Concept I_____
Concept II_____
Concept III_____
Concept IV_____
Concept V_____
Concept VI_____
Concept VII_____
Concept VIII_____
Concept IX_____
Concept X_____
Concept XI_____
Concept XII_____

Ever done a 180? This is a good path.

other customs

Meeting Format:

Since each Humane Way group is independent and sovereign, meeting formats will greatly vary. However, there are two general sources of inspiration for formats: 1) the 12 Step meeting formats, which themselves are a richly varied tradition, and 2) existing Anthroposophic meeting formats, such as the study group format. If an existing Anthroposophic group were to join Humane Way, the only essential change in format would be that the Four Legacies find a place in the meeting, at least in some small way.

Funding:

From the start, we instill a tradition of passing the hat at each meeting. No one is required to donate, but we do have expenses. These coins and dollars really add up. Like other Fellowships, Humane Way has (non-mandatory) guidelines for splitting the money with whatever Confederated Service Organisms the group is a member of. For example, AA suggests after group expenses are met (along with a prudent reserves) that the rest be donated via a 60:30:10 plan: 60% to a local Intergroup (if such exists), 30% to the World Service Office, and 10% to the local World Service District.

Like our predecessor Fellowships, no one who is not a member of the Fellowship may give money to Humane Way. We literally refuse money from any outside person, agency, or enterprise. And even within Humane Way, there are contribution limits...no living member may donate more than a certain amount per year. AA limits it to $3000 per person. Al-Anon limits it to no more than 1% of the World Service Office's budget. However, there is no limit to the amount that groups may donate to their confederated service organisms.

When I suggested that anthroposophy be funded in the same way, I was met with incredulousness, and suggested that the recovery Fellowships have a poverty mentality. Yet their "poverty mentality" has resulted in the most geographically pervasive spiritual movement in North America, and ever growing. Anthroposophy maintains a reportedly threadbare, largely deserted office in Ann Arbor, which is constantly begging for money. In contrast, AA has maintained a World Service Office in downtown Manhattan for decades. The other established Fellowships, such as Narcotics Anonymous and Overeaters Anonymous, maintain flourishing offices as well. All of this through freely-given, small-scale donations and literature sales. Humane Way may apply a small mark-up to hard copies of its literature, but the texts are also posted as open source documents to read online.

Credit for past actions?

Some might wonder: if I've already done the Twelve Steps before, or if I've already studied and practiced Anthropsophy, do I skip over some of the Quests?

The pathway through the Twelve Quests is an organic, whole experience. Even if we've done the Steps before, then some other habit or hindrance can be dealt with by another run through the Steps. And the anthroposophic content will appear differently when approached in a systemic twelvefold way.

Sponsors:

Humane Way continues to evolve the tradition of Personal Sponsor. In Humane Way, we are encouraged to connect with a sponsor who has qualities or experience that we want for ourself. This makes the Humane Way experience personal and individualized. Sponsors typically serve as a guide or sounding board as the member traverses the path of the 180 Actions. Yet no one is required to have a sponsor. The word "sponsor" is found nowhere in the Four Legacies.

Sponsorship can be as flexible as firm as the Wayfarer wishes. Two friends might co-sponsor each other. The "sponsor" could be called by other names, such as "recovery partner" or "program buddy" or "mentor." Likewise, there might be other terms for "sponsee" or "sponsoree", such as "protégé." One person might have more than one sponsor, asking the sponsors to serve in different roles, such as "step sponsor", "traditions sponsor", "service sponsor", "meditation sponsor", a "check-in sponsor" with whom the Wayfarer feels comfortable sharing about their daily travails, or an "adventure sponsor" or "quest sponsor" for a particular Adventure or Quest.

Instilling a a culture of personal sponsorship will provide a way for anthroposophy to become more personable, transmittable, and service-oriented. We all possess gems and treasures of experience that someone else in the world is looking for, and now we will have a meaningful way to share these in a one-on-one, informal, deprofessionalized context. Every Wayfarer—even ones who are on the First Step or First Quest—have a message to bear: their own experience.

A word about "Sponsorism." While the "hard-line" faction of traditionalist sponsorship—with lineage-based "pigeon-keepers"—is welcome to unfold also in Humane Way, measures are taken to guard from any monopolistic interpretation of the sponsorship role. Al-Anon World Services has itself recently issued statements along these lines. Humane Way is about individual initiative and higher power, moreso than Jesuitical/guru-ish "sponsorism." At the same time, we recognize that some persons flourish in the hardline customs. The whole spectrum of sponsorship would be welcome in Humane Way. Sponsoring is a beautiful custom.

Membership Cards:
In some groups, it would be customary to offer a golden card to anyone who decides to consider themselves a member of Humane Way. The card is typically signed by the member themself, by the group secretary (if they are present), along with any Wayfarers who are in attendance at that meeting. The card can serve as a "birthday" reminder, since many Humane Way groups acknowledge and celebrate anniversaries of members. However, no card is necessary to enter any Humane Way event. Though our World Service Organism will be offering gold cards which can be purchased by groups at nominal cost, groups are encouraged to hand craft their own membership cards, even if it be simply hand-written on golden paper.

Medallions:
Some groups and sponsors acknowledge milestones by offering chips or medallions. Though plastic chips are widely available, wood and metal are more substantial; or, better yet would be tokens hand-crafted by an artsy member of the group. Medallions are usually offered along two lines: 1) marking months and years of membership in Humane Way. 2) marking progress through the 12 Steps, 12 Traditions study, 12 Concepts study, and 144 Adventures.

Celebrations and Festivals:
The main celebrations are: 1) Marking yearly membership anniversaries of home group members, 2) Celebrating a member's passage through 12th Step, and 3) Celebrating a member's passage through the 180th Action. We aim to offer Organic, sugar-free cake, or other living sweetness.

Some groups might also celebrate the Humanosophic festivals, such as the Festival of the Human Being (known in Anthroposophy as St. John's) and the Festival of Courageous Willingness (known in Anthroposophy as Michaelmas). Allied Way groups which apply the Four Legacies to other cultural streams might celebrate other festivals.

Open source:
From the very start, it is the custom of Humane Way to release all of its literature into the public domain immediately, and to refuse to trademark its name and symbols. Wayfarers are encouraged to self-publish their own stories of how they traversed the Four Legacies, including their own individual interpretation and adaptation of the path. Home Groups are welcome to publish their own local literature, such as compilations of the personal stories of past and present members. Basically, each Group is free to write its own Big Book/Basic Text to be used instead of, or alongside, the World Assembly-affirmed literature.

In the longer term, we seek to publish an open source English translation of Dr. S's *Total Output* (TO, also known as Gesamtausgabe/GA or Complete Works/CW), to be presented as a side-by-side German/English edition. And then to translate the TO into the other languages of humanity.

Revisable principles:
At the world-level, the Four Legacies can be revised by a ¾ approval of all registering Groups. (Groups and individuals are free to revise them at whim.) However, if there is explanatory text developed for the Twelve Concepts, it can be revised without holding a special vote. But future editions of the World Service Manual should contain a record of all past re-wordings and revisions of the Four Legacies. In contrast, how many anthroposophists can name how the 15 Foundational Statutes of the Anthroposophic Society have changed over the years? Change is good, but we need to be able to see where we've been.

***

service structure

Other than the individual human being, a Group—also known as a Home Group—is the only actual sovereign entity in Humane Way. What are now called "study groups" in Anthroposophy would, in Humane Way, each be a sovereign Group, with its own relationship with the World Service Organism, and own set of group officers (secretary, treasurer, and so forth).

Unlike in Anthroposophy, there are no National Societies in Humane Way. Every Home Group is equivalent in stature to anthroposophy's National Groups (a.k.a. "National Societies"), and to the General Society. Each set of rotating group officers is equivalent to the stature of the Vorstand of the General Anthroposophical Society.

Intergroups:
In localities where there are many Groups, they might form an Intergroup Service Organism. For example, the Berkshire-Taconic Branch of the Anthroposophic Society would, in Humane Way, be an Intergroup. Currently in Anthroposophy, the term "group" and "branch" are actually synonyms—it's just that some people mistakenly think that "branch" means "a group of study groups"; but actually "branch" and "group" are just two anthroposophical terms for what its predecessor (the Theosophical Society) called "lodges." A "branch" and "group" are registered as the same kind of entity in the meeting lists of the National Society.

As in the existing Fellowships, there could be instances where a single Group, with a single set of group officers, hosts multiple meetings on various days of the week. In those cases, the word "Group" is not synonymous with a "meeting." But this is not expected to be the norm. Because the general aim is for decentralization, so as to cultivate individuality, reponsibility, and identity at the most granular, localized, meeting-sized scale.

From Hierarchy to Lowerarchy:
Humane Way is composed of a myriad of upside-down pyramids. Instead of hierarchies, these are "lowerarchies." (We realize that the word "hierarchy" doesn't really mean "higher-archy", but means "holy rule", but the word does have some tired connotations. The authentic "sacred governance" of today is decentralized and egalitarian.) Though the 12 Step Fellowships are instilled with the lowerarchy principle, there is still an unconscious systemic tendency in the Fellowships toward forming one big upside down pyramid, in the name of regularization and standardization, with everything united into a monolithic World Servic e Structure. It becomes one big big pyramid, which wields a formative force on the groups; for example, the tendency toward a strict adherence to Conference-Approved literature, when historically, many groups wrote their own local literature. In contrast, in Humane Way, each group is its own independent upside-down pyramid, and the World Service Organism is only one of many confederated service organisms which those sovereign pyramids may use to carry the Group's message. While Humane Way does propagate a specific formative force—the Four Legacies—our radically decentralized service organism encourages incredible diversity. We are not here to churn out World Conference-Approved cooke-cutter franchises.

Mutual registration:
Unlike in the existing Fellowships, a Humane Way group doesn't "register" with a confederated service organism, rather, a group and the service organism (which is a tool of all the groups who have delegated certain responsibilities into the service organism) may choose to mutually acknowledge each other, and to thereby mutually register each other. In a similar way that the service organism assigns a registration number to each member group, each group typically assigns each of its service organisms a number.

World Service Regions, Areas, and Districts:
Like AA, the World Service Organism of Humane Way includes World Service Regions, World Service Areas, and World Service Districts. As in Al-Anon, the Areas are, from the outset, based on the North American states and provinces, and their equivalent in other continents, roughly based on a similar size and population. For example, each French region, each German federal state, each Russian federal subject, and each Chinese provincial-level division is a World Service Area. The District boundaries are based on the North American county-level units, and their equivalent in other continents. Unlike in AA, the Areas and Districts cover the whole earth from the start. Whereas in AA, the General Service Boards of foreign nation-states are not integrated into the so-called "World Service Conference"...which is really only a "US-Canada-The Bahamas-Puerto Rico-U.S. Virgin Islands-British Virgin Islands-Antigua-St. Maarten-Cayman Islands Service Conference"

"Bill's early vision was of a worldwide structure. However the Conference structures in countries outside of the U.S./Canada evolved as autonomous entities."

—AA Ireland

But in Humane Way, the boundaries of nation-states do not block out the World Service Organism. For example, each Central American nation-state is a single World Service Area. Groups interested in forming a service organism based on a nation-state's boundaries would be free to form a "Zonal Service Organism" (ZSO), but the ZSOs are not a part of the World Service Organism, as such.

Many kinds of Confederated Service Organisms:
Unlike most of the Fellowships, Humane Way clarifies that the World Service Organism is but one of many service organisms. AA preserves some distinction between the World Service organs (Areas and Districts) and independent Intergroups (a.k.a. Central Offices), but in the newer Fellowships, this distinction is usually lost and collapsed into a single hierarchy; for example, in Overeaters Anonymous, "Intergroups" are just the name for the closest level of World Service hierarchy, similar to AA's World Service Districts. Humane Way fully untangles this. The only thing "special" about the WSO is that it is conceived as the most geographically and thematically encompassing service organism. Its Areas and Districts are formed primarily to serve as organs of communication between the group leadership and the world leadership. In contrast, Intergroup Service Organisms (IGSOs) are formed by groups on an ad-hoc basis, to service specific needs which are not necessarily met by the World Service Areas and Districts. A IGSO service area may cover a completely different geography than the World Service Areas and Districts. But the WSO is not "above" the other service organisms. The Area and District world service organs may exist alongside any number of other confederated service organisms formed by two or more groups, including (but not limited to):

▼ Intergroup Service Organisms (IGSOs): Geographic service organisms which arise outside of the WSO's Area and District framework.
▼ Zonal Service Organisms (ZSOs): 193 service organisms which are intentionally crafted to serve as an interface with the 193 legal jurisdictions (nation-states). As with any service organism, ZSOs are voluntary confederations of sovereign groups, and have no monopoly on Humane Way services. ZSOs are just one of many potential service organisms with which a group might choose to affiliate. In some localities, other kinds of service organisms (such as the WSO's areas and districts, or language-based service organisms) might be more active than the ZSO.
▼ Continental Service Organisms (ConSOs): 6 or 7 continent-based service organisms. Serves as a healthy outlet for the tendency toward "continental supra-nationalism" as embodied in the European Union and African Union.
▼ Language Service Organisms (LSOs): Potentially a service organism for each of the 10,000 languages of humanity. Translates Humane Way literature.
▼ Special Composition Service Organisms (SCSOs): Service organisms based on special focuses, such as gender, sexual identity, or profession, but which are otherwise similar in content to mainline Humane Way meetings.
▼ Allied Way Service Organisms (AWSOs): Service organisms which marry the Four Legacies with the spiritual, conceptual, and aesthetic content of particular wisdom streams, such as religions, philosophies, worldviews, and subcultures, to the extent that the wording of the Four Legacies is significantly adapted. Allied Way groups write their own Basic Text.

None of these service organisms are part of the WSO. These other kinds of service organisms are welcome to interact with the WSO via standing committees, such as the World+Intergroups Coordination Committee, the World+Languages Coordination Committee, and the World+Allied Ways Coordination Committee. Service organisms may also have their own relations with each other.

Relationship with Related Facilities:
Likewise, besides these confederations of groups, the WSO cultivates cooperation with Humane Way-inspired initiatives and enterprises which intentionally incorporate some aspect the Four Legacies into their operations. These are not Groups. Cooperation with such "related facilities" is embodied in the World+Inspired Initiatives and Enterprises Cooperation Commitee (W+II&E). This is similar to the existing Council of Anthroposophical Organizations. Such cooperation could be similarly embodied at other service scales; for example, a "Humane Way Intergroup in the Berkshire-Taconic Region" could have an "Berkshire-Taconic Intergroup+Inspired Initiatives & Enterprises Coordination Committee"

(IG+II&E) which serves as an interface between the local Home Groups (that is, Humane Way, as such) and various Humane Way inspired businesses and non-profit organizations.

Only Groups are members of the WSO:
Individual persons do not hold membership in the WSO (or other confederated service organisms), since confederations are composed only of Groups. However, scattered individuals could be represented in the World Service Organism by geographically-dispersed "Loners Groups", "Phone Groups", or "Online Groups" which "meet" via letter, phone, or internet. Within the world service structure, such virtual groups would comprise a non-geographic "Area." However, face-to-face meetings are encouraged—it only takes two persons to form a Group. (And don't tell anyone, but even a lone person is free to form a provisional Home Group composed of themself and their Higher Power, and to have that Group added to confederated meeting lists, as a way of getting a meeting started.) Even if there is only a single, small Group within a World Service Area, they are welcome and encouraged to send a World Service Delegate.

Humanocracy:
We adopt the Fellowships' "maddeningly democratic" custom of electing Group Representatives (GRs), District Representatives (DRs), and Area Representatives (ARs, also known as World Service Delegates). Because "democracy, as such" is the key principle of the political sphere, rather than the spiritual-cultural sphere, and because the word "democracy" has been so missused during the Century of Nightmare, we call our enculturated democracy by a fresh word: "humanocracy." Humanocracy keeps us interested in Humane Way in the long term. It provides life-long vistas of service and a widened consciousness of the geography of suffering and recovery. It promotes human agency and "ownership" of Humane Way. Humanocracy is a synthesis of democracy (each member holds an equal voice and vote in the Group Conscience) and republicanism (we entrust and empower individuals with service mandates).

Humane Way cannot help but come about through my individual gnosis at first—because someone first has to have the idea and start the impulse. But as soon as others arise and take up some semblance of this path, then it become co-authored. And then, after many adventures, we rotate out, and hand it off to the next generation.

Relationship with the Twelve Step Fellowships and with the Anthroposophic Organizations:
From the perspective of Humane Way, the Fellowships and the Anthro World serve as our "farm teams." Our Basic Text will explicitly commend Wayfarers to the spiritual tutelage of the Fellowships and the Anthro World. Nearly all of the Adventure ideas in our Provisional Basic Text will involve either the 12 Step rooms or the Anthro orgs.
The Fellowships are schools for passing through the Big Five Wounds (substance use, co-affliction, food, sex, and emotional recovery), and whatever other areas of life the 12 Steps have already penetrated (gambling, workaholism, tech addiction, and so forth).

Since 12 Step Fellowships hold to a policy of non-affiliation, there is no question of Humane Way actually affiliating with any existing Fellowship.

We are up front about how we intend from the outset to be a supersession of the Anthroposophical Society. We don't bow and scrape to the Anthroposophical Society or to the Goetheanum, visible or invisible. Of course any individual is free to be a member of the Society and Humane Way at the same time, yet Humane Way cannot heartily recommend membership in any of the National Societies or the General Society, since, honestly, these are not truly open to all social segments, given the membership fees. We do not favor the "pay to pray" approach. However, a Wayfarer is encouraged to be a member of a local Anthroposophic "society" (i.e. group or branch).

In the further future, the aim is to fully supersede the Society, and to invite her to converge with Humane Way and the 4x12 action-based principles.

Parallel Organisms:
Like its Anthroposophic and Theosophical predecessors, Humane Way would initiate parallel versions of existing organizations and cultural streams. For example, Theosophy founded its own version of the Christian religion, known as the Liberal Catholic Church. Subsequently, Anthroposophy did the same via The Christian Community: Movement for Religious Renewal. And both Theosophy and Anthroposophy formed parallel Freemasonry initiatives: Theosophy's Co-Freemasonry, and Anthroposophy's *Mystica Aeterna* service. Both were formed as distinct variations within two already-

existing masonic orders. Neither Theosophy nor Anthroposophy waited for any large segment of the existing Christian denominations, or of the Freemasonry lodges, before they went ahead an initiated their own parallel versions, and permeated the Christian religion and Freemasonry their own Theosophical or Anthroposophic aesthetic.

Humane Way takes this further. We would aim to intiate parallel versions of pretty much everything in life. Individuals and groups are encouraged to form parallel iterations of any organization or corporation or state which we interact with in daily life. Such parallel organisms might at first be symbolic and barely manifest. We form Four Legacies-based versions of any and all religions and philosophies, businesses, nations, and states. Some of these will remain symbolic indefinitely; others will blossom into fully manifest initiatives. Each individual Wayfarer might be a pioneer of a large number of symbolic or actual initiatives.

The custom of initiating Parallel Organisms serves these key purposes:

1) It helps each Wayfarer become aware of the archangels (organizations) we interact with on a daily basis.
2) It provides imaginal space for Wayfarers to picture: what would the most healthy, archetypal version of this organization, organization, or agency look like?
3) It instills a capacity for initiative in each Wayfarer. We aren't just passive recipients of the existing social order.
4) It provides a way for like-minded Wayfarers to find each other and collaborate on shared interests.
5) It is the vehicle by which Humane Way will permeate or supersede existing external structures, in a way that is imbued with the 4x12 principles, and warmed with siblinglike affection. We practice these principles in all our affairs, even in the most external affairs.

*"The real impulse of [the true social organism] consists in the realization of siblinghood in the widest sense of the term in the **external structure of society**. [...] One must first understand what is meant by siblinghood. On the physical plane **the present state-systems must be replaced throughout the whole world by institutions or organizations which are imbued with siblinghood**."*
—Rudolf St., GA185 (The word "brotherhood" is here refreshed as "siblinghood.")

Question: Would Humane Way also form parallel versions of the 12 Step Fellowships and Anthroposophical Organizations? Yes, wherever we can improve and extend existing efforts, we do. It is hard to imaging making a better version of AA anytime soon. Yet I myself already have sketched out a Humane Way version of Overeaters Anonymous, provisionally named The Chrysalis Felllowship, which uses the Fifth Quest wording as the "shared abstinence" definition. And it would be important for Humane Way to eventually inspire the formation of a new kind of Waldorf School which is pervaded with the principle of "freely you have received, freely give"—a third stream of sacramental Waldorf, besides the existing privatist (AWSNA) and governmentalist (Public Waldorf) factions. A Threefold Schoolhouse and Academy?

Individual Ways:
"Humanosophy", also known as "Humane Wisdom", is basically *Individuated Anthroposophy*.

Humane Way acknowledges that each individual has their own wisdom and way. In fact, even though it's not yet clearly acknowledged in the 12 Step Fellowships or in Anthroposophical society, that's the way it already is—even if someone followed the Big Book and Class Lessons exactly as written, and enacted nothing more or less than each dot and iota, each person is really enacting their own version of the Twelve Steps and Class Lessons. In fact, authentic spiritual teachings in this age can only be manifest in an individual way. Otherwise we would literally be robots and computers.

In Humane Way, we not only acknowledge that, we faciliate that and embody it. Because Humane Way texts are open source, each individual is encouraged to revise and adapt the Four Legacies to tell exactly how *they* traversed the path, in their own words. A person is even free to develop an Allied Way with a different name, as "John D's Way" (or whatever they wish to name their spiritual experience). Humane Way is glad for individuated versions of the Four Legacies to spread and multiply, resulting in a countless variety of allied groups and confederated service organisms. As long as some iteration of the Four Legacies are central to that stream, then the Allied Way is encouraged to remain a full member of Humane Way. The only limit: if some semblance of the Four Legacies are no longer central, then the group or service organism could be asked by Humane Way-as-a-whole (the World Service Organism) to consider whether they want to remain listed as a Humane Way entity, or to form an outside, different Fellowship. When it comes down to it, since the name "Humane Way" is not trademarked, the most firm outward action which World Services would take is to delist the meeting. Humane Way does have boundaries and a membrane, but they are superbly encompassing.

allied ways

Humanosophy is *the wisdom of every human worldview, as permeated by the light of anthroposophic spiritual science*. Unlike Anthroposophy-as-it-exists, Humane Way is intentionally crafted to be able to be re-skinned and re-clothed in the conceptual and aesthetic fabric of any cultural stream of humanity, whether it be a religion, philosophy, nationality, or subculture. Even fictive memes can serve as the basis of an Allied Way, since that's what the soul world is made of: imaginal substance.

An Allied Way is a Humane Way group which intentionally melds the Four Legacies principles to a specific wisdom tradition or subculture. Such an Allied Way group would author a provisional basic text which adapts the Four Legacies to their own terminology, and which gives examples and sources from that specific tradition, especially as seen in the light of the AA principles and anthroposophy. As more and more persons from that tradition work through the Four Legacies, their stories could be incorporated into that Allied Way text. When two or more such groups form, they could initiate a confederated service organism. Such groups are full members of Humane Way, and would listed in a specific way on World Services meeting lists, so that interested persons could seek them out, and disinterested persons could avoid that meeting. The World Service Organism maintains a relationship with Allied Way confederate service organisms via a standing World+Allied Ways Coordination Council.

All it takes to form an Allied Way is to form a group which intends to adapt the Four Legacies to a particular cultural stream. The group might start with an enculturated version of the Twelve Steps (the recent Mormon adaptation is a good example), and then write a basic text later. Or Wayfaring authors might write the book first, and then start a group.

An Allied Way basic text would feature:
▼ A re-languaging of the 12 Steps, Traditions, Concepts, and Quests. For example, an explicitly Christian permeation would write "Christ Jesus" in place of "Higher Power." A Jewish Way group would write: "YWH" or "Adonai", a Muslim Way "Allah", and so forth. The adaptation could be as simple as a change in names, or the wording could be thoroughly re-cast. For example, a Jehovah's Witnesses Way would cultivate:
  ∇ Jehovah's Recovery (Quests 1 through 5)
  ∇ Jehovasophy / Jehovah's Wisdom (Quest 6)
  ∇ Jehovah's Mysteries (Quest 7)
  ∇ Jehovah's Science (Quest 8)
  ∇ Jehovah's Arts (Quest 9)
  ∇ Jehovah's Social Renewal (Quests 10 through 12)
  While a Wiccan Way would cultivate:
  ∇ Wiccan Recovery (Quests 1 through 5)
  ∇ Wiccanosophy / Wiccan Wisdom (Quest 6)
  ∇ Wiccan Mysteries (Quest 7)
  ∇ Wiccan Science (Quest 8)
  ∇ Wiccan Arts (Quest 9)
  ∇ Wiccan Social Renewal (Quests 10 through 12)
  All of this would be explicitly permeated with the warm will of Recovery and the clear light of Anthroposophy.
▼ One or more personal stories from Wayfarers who have traversed the Four Legacies and who identify with that Allied Way. As more and more persons in that stream work through the Legacies, more stories might be added to the book.
▼ Adventure ideas, such as source texts and overviews of existing initiatives from that cultural stream which relate to the 12 Steps and to Anthroposophy, within the twelve spheres of life of the Twelve Quests.
▼ New texts written by Wayfarers which attempt to marry that cultural stream to the light of the Twelve Steps and Humane Wisdom.

Some might try to re-embody entire streams by giving examples from the entire spectrum of past and present denominational offshoots. Others might embody only a single splinter stream (such as a denomination) or the teachings of a single figure, such as St. Francis. Both lumping and splitting are valid approaches.

Since the group is the only sovereign social entity in Humane Way, a single group might use more than one Basic Text and might be a member of multiple Confederated Service Organisms, from multiple streams of Humane Way. For example, a Christian Way group might sometimes read from the mainline Humane Way text, sometimes from one of several Christian Way texts written by various Wayfarers, and sometimes from a specific denominational text with which they identify (e.g. an Anglican/Episcopal Way text). For popular streams (such as Christianity or Yoga), various Wayfarers or service organisms might write "competing" basic texts. That's all well and good.

To prime the imaginal juices, here's a big list of some of the possibilities. Do you see one which you would like to pioneer? The harvest is plentiful, but the workers are few.

Christian ways:
▼   Golgothan Way—Movement for Christian Recovery and Renewal. An example of a "lumping" stream which tries to re-embody all streams of Christianity. Summarizes and encompasses all the way from the Apostolic Church to the Gnostic Churches to the Assyrian Church (the oldest continuously embodied offshoot) to Orthodoxy, Catholicism, and Protestantism, to the new Nontrinitarian Churches (Jehovah's Witness, Mormon), and to the modern Independent Churches (Rock Solid in Hudson); with the Johannine CC rites and Emil Bock's writings service as central inspirations and touchstones. We develop our own Bible which includes all apocryphal books which any traditional denomination has included in their Bible, but translated and rendered in the light of humanosophy.
▼   Biblical Way—Movement for Evangelical Recovery and Renewal
▼   Via Petrinī • Petrine Way—Movement for (Roman) Catholic Recovery and Renewal. See: *The Greater and Lesser Mysteries of Christianity: The Complementary Paths of Anthroposophy and Catholicism* by Ron MacFarlane.
▼   Andréou Hodós • Andrean Way—Movement for (Eastern/Byzantine) Orthodox Recovery and Renewal
▼   Cyrillian Way—Movement for Oriental Orthodox Recovery and Renewal. (A friend here showed me some artifacts from the Ethiopian Orthodox church. Two friends have visited here who are from an Armenian Orthodox background.)
▼   Marcan Way—Movement for Coptic Orthodox Recovery and Renewal
▼   Philippine Way—Movement for Ethiopian Orthodox Tewahedo Recovery and Renewal
▼   Frumentian Way— Movement for Eritrean Orthodox Tewahedo Recovery and Renewal
▼   Gregorian Way—Movement for Armenian Apostolic Recovery and Renewal
▼   Jacobite (or Theophoric) Way—Movement for Syriac Orthodox Recovery and Renewal
▼   Thomine (or Jacobite or Nasrani) Way—Movement for Malankara Orthodox Syrian Recovery and Renewal
▼   Antiochene Way—Movement for Assyrian Christian Recovery and Renewal
▼   The Ninety-Five Theses (or Wittenbergian) Way—Movement for Lutheran Recovery and Renewal
▼   Wesleyan Way—Movement for Methodist Recovery and Renewal. *"Some will think that Steiner has said too much of Christ as the explanation of the whole universe; some, that he has said too little of Jesus, as the Redeemer of a small but important part of that universe, the individual soul. But it cannot be denied that he sees, in the activity manifested once for all in Jesus, a guide for action in every sphere and interest of life, economic and social, political and educational."* —W.F. Lofthouse, theologian at the Handsworth Methodist Theological College, and President of the Wesleyan Conference, The *Quarterly Review*, London, January 1923.
▼   Knoxian Way—Movement for Presbyterian Recovery and Renewal
▼   Zwinglian Way—Movement for Swiss Reformed Recovery and Renewal
▼   Canterburian Way—Movement for Anglican/Episcopal Recovery and Renewal. *"The four points on which the O.C.M. places—in the present situation—its main emphasis: 1) A Christian Social Order which will be threefold as elucidated by Rudolf Steiner. [...] 4) The promulgation of spiritual science as the exposure of the false materialistic science of to-day."* —Jack Bucknall, priest of the Church of England, with the Order of the Church Militant, 1944
▼   Inner Light Way—Movement for Quaker Recovery and Renewal
▼   Jehovah's Way—Movement for Witness (or Watchtower) Recovery and Renewal. (Dr. S spoke obliquely about the spirit of Jehovah's Witness in its earlier manifestation as the ancient Mexican god Tezcatlipoka.)
▼   Angel Moroni Way—Movement for Mormon Recovery and Renewal. Glimpses of a humanosophically-enhanced Mormon Way:

"After spending a few days in Concho, Arizona, where I got baptized and ordained to the Priesthood, I went on a tour of Monument Valley. [...]As I was waiting for my flight, I found the following quote in a novel I picked up: "<u>Man is at the same time a fallen God and a God in the becoming</u>" (Rudolf Steiner)."You cannot get more Mormon than that!" "To paraphrase Joseph Smith: Truth is truth, no matter what its source is. So, if Rudolf Steiner, the Pope or the Devil share some truth, I will accept it if/when I am satisfied it is the truth. Being a Fundamentalist does not mean I have to be closed-minded. Our faith, after all, does not have any creed." "Rudolf Steiner was a Rosicrucian. I do not know enough about that society to make any comments, but I know Rosicrucianism shares similarities with Masonic and Mormon teachings. Why those similarities?"* —"<u>Rudolf Steiner and Joseph Smith</u>", blog entry from "Mormon(s) of another kind", 2012.

"In many ways, Julene traveled a traditional path through Mormonism as she raised her children, but when her oldest son decided to be done with the church rather than depart on a mission as she was expecting, she began a journey that lead her toward a world of thought filled with the Divine Feminine" "From the roots given to her subtly by her mother, Julene built further with the Christ-centered philosophy of anthroposophy created by Rudolf Steiner, as she moved toward re-enthroning Sophia in her spiritual life and seeking for a true balance between the Divine Feminine and the Divine Masculine." —Introduction to Julene Humes' "Daughters of Mormonism" podcast "<u>If any of you lack Sophia...</u>", 2011. Julene H. is the author of <u>Anthroposophy and Mormonism: Two Tributaries of The Secret Stream</u>.

"Though he was also a social and educational reformer, an architect, and a philosopher, he is most well-known as a mystic, esotericist, and founder of the spiritual movement called anthroposophy. And what a mystic he is.... He talks about things ranging from auras to chakras to the spiritual nature of dreams, and even though they might strike the modern person as a bit "out there," his writings have done more than most mystical works to satisfy both my intellect and my spiritual sensibilities." "All rambling aside, I wanted to use this post to talk about a book of his I just finished: How to Know Higher Worlds. *[...] It's a really good book; you should all read it. I felt the Spirit quite a lot while reading it, so I feel that it's true in its essence."* —Christian James Swenson, "<u>Journals of a Mormon Mystic</u>", 2015.

- ▼ Seventh-day Way—Movement for Adventist Recovery and Renewal
- ▼ Calvinian Way—Movement for Reformed Recovery and Renewal
- ▼ Menno Simmons Way—Movement for Mennonite Recovery and Renewal
- ▼ Jakob Ammann Way—Movement for Amish Recovery and Renewal
- ▼ Jakob Hutter Way—Movement for Hutterite Recovery and Renewal
- ▼ Eberhard Arnold Way—Movement for Bruderhof Recovery and Renewal
- ▼ Gnosis Way—Movement for Gnostic Recovery and Renewal
- ▼ Divine Mind Way—Movement for Christian Scientist Recovery and Renewal
- ▼ Via Nova Hierosolyma • New Jerusalem Way—Movement for Swedenborgian Recovery and Renewal
- ▼ The Se-Baptist Way—Movement for Baptist Recovery and Renewal
- ▼ The Cambridge Platform (or Puritan) Way—Movement for Congregationalist Recovery and Renewal
- ▼ Restoration Way—Movement for Church of Christ Recovery and Renewal
- ▼ Blood and Fire Way—Movement for Salvation Army Recovery and Renewal
- ▼ Via Fratrum—Movement for Moravian Recovery and Renewal
- ▼ Pentecostal Way
- ▼ Holiness Way
- ▼ Church of God Way
- ▼ Nazarene Way
- ▼ The Divine Principle Way—Movement for Unificationist Recovery and Renewal

Actually all of Humane Way, and all of its Allied Ways, strive to be "Golgothan" and "Christic" in the moral-transformative sense, but not all streams of Humane Way use Christian terminology.

Christian Way groups, like other Humane Way groups, are ultra-congregationalist. Only individuals and congregations (groups) are sovereign. A congregation (which, in Humane Way, is equivalent to an independent church) could belong to none, one, or multiple Confederal Service Organisms. For example, a group might choose to affiliate with an all-encompassing "Golgothan Way" CSO, along with whichever "church stream(s)" (based on the historical "denominations") they identify with. Ultra-congregationalism actually allows for more actual ecumenism than the existing denominational model, and also goes beyond the existing independent church model, since a group/congregation could participate in multiple confederations at the same time while still keeping its congregational singularity. Furthermore, there is a conscious communion with all other human cultural streams within Humane Way via the Four Legacies.

"If we ask how Jesus lived his life, we are faced with a paradox. There is a strange wildness in what he does that defies our logic. On the other hand, he is not out of control, a 'reed tossed by the wind.' We feel that his wildness comes from his faithfulness to an order that we can only guess at – an order at odds with the order we try to impose upon life. [...]

*"The crossroads is a fitting image for the work of Christ. {...} He appears in history and in life as something that intersects with human lives, **and human history, questioning their direction, bringing newness of life along with danger and risk.** [...] Christ's wildness, his lack of conformity to the order we know and expect, is not arbitrary, but stems from a different order. Christ is a 'way' that crosses our own, introducing us to a cosmic past and **opening up a future greater than our imaginings.**"*

—Tom Ravetz, "Finding Ourselves at the Crossroads",
Perspectives journal of the Christian Community, September-November 1999.

Ways of East Asian and South Asian origin (religious or martial arts-based):

▼ Amma Love Way (I saw a photo of her around here.)
▼ Bodhi Maggo • Awakening Way—Movement for Buddhadharmic Recovery and Renewal (This would be an all-encompassing synthesis of Theravāda, Mahayana, Vajrayana and Western Buddhism, cast in the light of the 12 Steps and Anthroposophy. We would develop our own Canon which includes all canonical texts from all those traditions, along with the Gospel of Luke and Dr. S's lectures on Buddhism. A renewal of specific lineages of Buddhism would also be possible.)
▼ Thegpa Rimpa Dgu • Nine Sequential Ways—Movement for Bön Recovery and Renewal (I saw a Bön image posted on a friend's refrigerator here in the Berkshire-Taconic Homeland.)
▼ Vaidik Mārga • Vedic Way—Movement for Hindu Recovery and Renewal
▼ Dàodé Dàolù • The Way and Virtue Way—Movement for Taoist Recovery and Renewal
▼ Rú Dàolù • Way of the Scholar—Movement for Confucian Recovery and Renewal
▼ Ik Onkar Māraga • Way of the One Supreme Reality—Movement for Sikh Recovery and Renewal
▼ Kami No Michi • Way of the Gods—Movement for Shinto Recovery and Renewal
▼ Moksha Mārga • Way to Liberation—Movement for Jain Recovery and Renewal
▼ Krishna Consciousness Way—Movement for Hare Krishna Recovery and Renewal
▼ Shindo (Shin Gil?)—Movement for Muist (Ancient Korean) Recovery and Renewal
▼ Uttara Mīmāṃsā Mārga • Higher Enquiry Way—Movement for Vedānta Recovery and Renewal (Friends have shared with me about Vedanta.)
▼ Whispered Transmission Way—Movement for Kagyu Recovery and Renewal
▼ Paccakkha Maggo • Insight Way—Movement for Vipassanā Recovery and Renewal
▼ Yoga & Health Way—Movement for Kripalu Recovery and Renewal
▼ Yoga Way—Movement for Samādhic Recovery and Renewal
▼ The Sacred Way of Warriorship—Movement for Shambhalian Recovery and Renewal
▼ Aikido Way
▼ Judo Way
▼ Karate Way
▼ Taekwondo Way
▼ Tai Chi Way
▼ Qigong Way
▼ Kung Fu Way
▼ Dalai Lama Way—centered on the person of Tenzin Gyatso, the 14th Dalai Lama, rather than on Tibetan Buddhism as a whole.

*"Now learn a parable of the **fig tree**; When his branch is yet tender, and putteth forth leaves, ye know that summer is nigh:*
"So likewise ye, when ye shall see all these things, know that it is near, even at the doors."

—The Representative of Humanity, speaking in the Gospel of Matthew: 24:32–33

Ways of Middle Eastern origin:

▼ Derekh Sinay • Sinaïc Way—Movement for Jewish Recovery and Renewal. Seeks to embody the most beautiful and virtuous traditions from all branches of Judaism, as held in the warmth and light of the Twelve Steps and Anthroposophy. Resource: *Judaism and Anthroposophy* by John Howe (ed.). *"Elijah took twelve stones [...] With the stones he built an altar in the name of the LORD"* —The Book of Kings

▼ Ṭarīq al-Fard • The Singular Way—Movement for Islamic Recovery and Renewal. (Resources: SEKEM's work, *Islam in relation to the Christ impulse: a search for reconciliation between Christianity and Islam : an anthroposophic inquiry* by Andrei Younis, *The Impulse of Freedom in Islam* by John Van Schaik, Christine Gruwez and Cilia Ter Horst, *Christianity and Islam* by Rudolf Frieling.)

▼ Ráh Bahá'í • Way of Glory—Movement for Bahá'í Recovery and Renewal

▼ Ṭarīq al-Muwaḥḥidun • Monotheist Way—Movement for Druze Recovery and Renewal

▼ Way of Light—Movement for Manichæan Recovery and Renewal. (Resource: Christine Gruwez's work)

▼ Ráh Ormazd • Ahura Mazdao Way—Movement for Zoroastrian Recovery and Renewal (Resource: E.E.Pfeiffer's *Zarathustrian Way* booklet.)

▼ Sabian Way

▼ Mandæan Way

▼ Yazidi Way

Early western ways (occult, legendary, and belletristic):

▼ Trismegistic Way—Movement for Hermetic Recovery and Renewal through Alchemy, Astrology, and Theurgy

▼ Star Wisdom Way—Movement for Astrological Recovery and Renewal

▼ Avalon Way—Movement for Arthurian Recovery and Renewal

▼ Paladin Way—Movement for Carolingian Recovery and Renewal

▼ Percival Way—Movement for Grail Recovery and Renewal

▼ Via Roseæ Crucis (or Via Christiani Rosenkreuz)—Movement for Rosicrucian Recovery and Renewal

▼ The Prophecies Way—Movement for Nostradamic Recovery and Renewal

▼ Goethean Way

▼ Schiller Way

▼ Weimar Classicism Way (includes Goethe, Schiller, and others)

▼ Novalis Way

▼ Romantic Way (includes Novalis, Keats, Shelley, and others)

▼ William Blake Way

Western philosophical ways:

▼ Pythagorean Way

▼ Platonic Way

▼ Aristotelean Way

▼ Kantian Way

▼ German Idealist Way (includes Fichte, Hegel, and others)

▼ Hegelian Way

▼ Fichtean Way

▼ Nietzschean Way

▼ William James Way—Movement for Pragmatic Recovery and Renewal. 'Experiential Truth' and 'Realized Idealism.'

▼ Philosopher's Way (an all-encompassing, "lumper" way)

New spiritual ways:

▼ Blavatskyan Way—Movement for Theosophical Recovery and Renewal

▼ Unitarian Way—Movement for Universalist Recovery and Renewal

▼ The Over-Soul Way—Movement for American Transcendentalist Recovery and Renewal. More than one Anthroposophist has suggested that American anthroposophy be re-centered on Emerson and the Transcendentalists. I agree that this would be a good endeavor. But to most Americans, Emerson is hardly more familiar than Goethe or Solovyov. In contrast, millions of Americans seriously strive within 12 Step spirituality every day. Such a Transcendentalist Way would approach the works of Emerson, Thoreau, the Alcotts, and Margaret Fuller via a 12 Step and Anthroposophical framework.

- ▼ Dianetics Way—Movement for Scientological Recovery and Renewal
- ▼ Pagan Witchcraft Way—Movement for Wiccan Recovery and Renewal
- ▼ Living Ethics Way—Movement for Agni Yoga Recovery and Renewal
- ▼ Incarnational Spirituality Way—Movement for Lorian Recovery and Renewal. *"Dear Travis, David read your introduction to the work you are engaging to bringing together New Age Communities. He passed along the response that the projects to which he is currently dedicated don't leave him with the time or energy to take on any new commitments. However, he is appreciative of your invitation and certainly wishes you well and every success in this endeavor. with regards, Freya Secrest, Lorian Association"* email correspondence, June 13th, 2012.
- ▼ The Way of Socrates—Movement for Peaceful Warrior Recovery and Renewal
- ▼ Anastasia Way—Movement for Ringing Cedars Recovery and Renewal
- ▼ Psychonaut Way—Movement for New Edge Recovery and Renewal
- ▼ Research and Enlightenment Way (REW)—Movement for Caycean Recovery and Renewal. (I heard a friend here talk about his medical offerings. An early Think OutWorder friend is a Caycean. Cayce spoke for the Threefold Republic: Q: *"Is it within the bounds of possibility that the threefold social order of Rudolf Steiner can be brought about in this country?"* A: *"These are the characters of activities of social order, of social justice,—yes. ...The social order, the religious order, the economic order must all be for ONE God!"* —Reading #3976-24, July, 16, 1939. In regard to Humane Way's aspirations: Q: *"How soon [till the Second Coming]?"* A: *"When those who belong to Him have made His way clear for Him to come."* —Reading #262-49 July 9, 1933, quoted in (Christian Community priest) Carl Stegmann's *Other America,* Part II, p. 25.
- ▼ The Fourth Way—Movement for Gurdjieffian Recovery and Renewal. (I have been friends with Gurdjieffian people here in the Berkshire-Taconic Homeland.)
- ▼ Thelema Way—Movement for Crowleyan Recovery and Renewal
- ▼ Satanic Way—Movement for LaVeyan Recovery and Renewal. (Yes it can be done. It's just that its Steps guide the Satanic Wayfarer to indulge in the Lower Powers (alcohol and so forth) for as long as one will, until it's no longer fun. That's when the Higher Power comes in. That's what addicts and humanity do anyway. And a LaVeyan Satanist gave a fine talk at an Anthroposophic conference I was at. Satanists have been on the forefront of offering protection to Muslim Americans.)
- ▼ Byalo Bratsvo Peut • White Brotherhood (or Brotherhood of Light) Way—Movement for Deunovian Recovery and Renewal
- ▼ Be Here Now Way—Movement for Recovery and Renewal through the Teachings of Neem Karoli Baba and Ram Dass
- ▼ Quan Yin Way—Movement for Suma Ching Hai Recovery and Renewal
- ▼ Integral Way—Movement for Wilburian Recovery and Renewal
- ▼ Church Universal and Triumphant Way
- ▼ Eckankar Way
- ▼ Ageless Wisdom Way—Movement for Baileyan Recovery and Renewal. *"How He will come, in what way, is not certain. The right moment has not yet come, and the manner of His Appearing is not determined." "The Son of God is on His way, and He is not coming alone. His pioneers are already here, and the plan they must follow has already been made and is clear."* –quoted in (Christian Community priest) Carl Stegmann's *Other America*, Part II, pp. 24-25.
- ▼ I AM Way—Movement for Saint Germain Recovery and Renewal
- ▼ Pathless Way—Movement for Krishnamurti Recovery and Renewal
- ▼ Course in Miracles Way
- ▼ New Thought Way
- ▼ Cosmo-Conception Way—Movement for Max Heindel's Rosicrucian Recovery and Renewal
- ▼ Roza Mira Way—Movement for Andreevian Recovery and Renewal
- ▼ Right Use of Will (RUOW) Way (or Ceanne DeRohan Way) (A friend shared with me from this spiritual tradition.)
- ▼ New Age Way (an all-encompassing "lumper" of many streams)
- ▼ Tombergian Way—Movement for Recovery and Renewal through *Meditations on the Tarot*
- ▼ Tony Robbins Way

Ethnic-centered/folk ways:
- ▼ Njia ya Afrika—Movement for African-Centered Recovery and Renewal
- ▼ Camino de Ochá—Movement for Santería Recovery and Renewal
- ▼ Mawu Way—Movement for Vodun Recovery and Renewal
- ▼ Orunmila Way—Movement for Ifá Recovery and Renewal

- ▼ I and I Way—Movement for Rastafari Icovery and Inewal
- ▼ Toltec Way—Movement for Nagualist Recovery and Renewal
- ▼ Slige Goídelach • Gaëlic Way—Movement for Ancient Gaëlic Recovery and Renewal (Irish: Slí Gaelach, first word pronounced "shlee.")
- ▼ Ffordd Frythoneg • Brittonic Way—Movement for Ancient Brittonic Recovery and Renewal (what is Proto-Brythonic for Brittonic Way?)
- ▼ Manidoo Miikana • Manitou Way—Movement for Algonquian Recovery and Renewal
- ▼ Twiskoniskaz Wegaz • Tuisconic Way—Movement for Ancient Northern Recovery and Renewal
- ▼ Km.t W3t • Kemetic Way—Movement for Ancient Egyptian Recovery and Renewal
- ▼ Slǎva Pǫtь—Movement for Ancient Slavic Recovery and Renewal
- ▼ Hetan Way—Movement for Ancient Armenian Recovery and Renewal. A friend visited here and we spoke about the one-sidedness of the resurgence of paganism in Armenia.
- ▼ Kituwa Nvnohi • Keetoowah Way—Movement for Cherokee Recovery and Renewal
- ▼ Orenda Way—Movement for Haudenosaunee Recovery and Renewal
- ▼ Wakan Ocaku—Movement for Oceti Sakowin Recovery and Renewal
- ▼ Dōdekátheon Hodós—Movement for Ancient Hellenic Recovery and Renewal
- ▼ Via Romana—Movement for Ancient Latinic Recovery and Renewal (http://www.novaroma.org/via_romana/
- ▼ Aestic(?) Way—Movement for Ancient Baltic Recovery and Renewal. An anthroposophist (Vydūnas / Wilhelm Storost) was the founder of modern Lithuanian and Prussian pagan renewal!
- ▼ Hyperborean Way—Movement for Ancient Uralic Recovery and Renewal (or save Hyperborean name as pan-Hyperborean, including east Siberian peoples?)
- ▼ Blue Sky Way—Movement for Tengrist Recovery and Renewal. *"Where shall we find a man who never drinks? If, however, such a man is found, he deserves every respect."* -Genghis Khan
- ▼ Great Mystery Way—Movement for Turtle Island-Centered Recovery and Renewal. (An all-encompassing way serving all indigenous North American cultures.)
- ▼ Dreamtime Way—Movement for Aboriginal Australian-Centered Recovery and Renewal
- ▼ Inti Way—Movement for Tuwantinsuyu-Centered Recovery and Renewal
- ▼ Anahuac Way—Movement for Mēxihcah-Centered Recovery and Renewal
- ▼ Inuit Way
- ▼ Hawaiki Way—Movement for Polynesian-Centered Recovery and Renewal
- ▼ Melanesian Way
- ▼ Amazonian Way
- ▼ Maya Way
- ▼ Adivasi Way—Movement for Indigenous South Asian Recovery and Renewal
- ▼ Hyperborean Way—Movement for Indigenous Siberian Recovery and Renewal
- ▼ Nyambe Way—Movement for African Animist Recovery and Renewal. (Encompassing all African indigenous mysteries. Source: Orland Bishop, since he has been initiated into indigenous African mysteries.)
- ▼ Ancient Gaulish Way
- ▼ Celtic Way (A "lumper" way serving Brittonic, Gaelic, Gaulish, and other Celtic-identifying streams.)
- ▼ Ancient Illyrian Way
- ▼ Ancient Etruscan Way
- ▼ Ancient Phoenician Way
- ▼ Ancient Assyrian Way
- ▼ Ancient Sumerian Way
- ▼ Ancient Malay Way
- ▼ Golden Land Way (All pre-Islamic, pre-Buddhist, pre-Hindu religions of Southeast Asia.)
- ▼ Ancient Semitic Way ("pagan" Semitic culture: Jewish, Arab, Canaanite, Phoenician, Aramean, Ethiopic, Assyrian)
- ▼ Ancient Iberian Way
- ▼ Ancient Libyan Way (pre-Muslim Berber and Guanche pagan culture)
- ▼ Ancient Hittite Way
- ▼ Ancient Caucasus Way
- ▼ Ancient Thracian Way (and Phrygian, Getic, and Dacian)

Imaginal/fictive/literary ways: Some fictive-based Allied Ways might focus on the author and all their works, while others might be based on a specific title or series. For example, there might be a C.S. Lewis Way basic text which contains Adventure ideas pulled from all of Lewis' fictional and non-fictional corpus. But someone else might write a Narnia Way basic text which only includes examples from that series. And so there might be C.S. Lewis Way groups and Narnia Way groups, each with their own separate Confederated Service Organism. However, some of the groups might use both texts, and belong to both service organisms. Not to mention that more than one Wayfarer might write "competing" texts on the same subject—even with the exact same title! There could also be Basic Texts covering an entire genre (Science Fiction Way) or medium (Film Way).

As for copyright issues—there already exists a minor industry of philosophical and religious books about various fictive worlds, which are not licensed by the "intellectual property"-holder, such as *The Gospel According to Star Wars* and *The Dharma of Star Wars*. Our basic texts would be along those lines, and would go as far as possible without using actually infringing materials (photos, long quotes). Perhaps in the further future, there could be officially licensed adaptations.

▼ Shakespearean Way—Movement for Recovery and Renewal through the Dramatic Worlds of the Bard
▼ Tië Ardó—Movement for Recovery, Escape, and Consolation through J.R.R. Tolkien's Middle-earth Legendarium
▼ Way of the Force—Movement for the Hero's Journey and for the Alliance to Restore the Republic (or Movement for Recovery and Renewal through George Lucas' Star Wars Universe). Resources: "Source of the Force: The True Back Story About Why It Became The World's Newest Religion" by neo-anthroposophist Douglas Gabriel; and the related article "Starkillers and Ahriman: How a Steiner Think Tank Rewrote Star Wars."
▼ Aslan's Way—Movement for Recovery and Renewal through C.S. Lewis' Chronicles of Narnia
▼ Master of Death Way—Movement for Recovery and Renewal through J.K. Rowling's Wizarding World of Harry Potter
▼ Triforce Way—Movement for Recovery and Renewal through Shigeru Miyamoto's and Takashi Tezuka's Legend of Zelda Universe
▼ Way of the Source—Movement for Recovery and Renewal through the Wachowski Brothers' Matrix Universe. Sources: "The Spiritual Matrix–An Anthroposophical Reading" by Seth Miller; Nicanor Perlas' "Importance of Social Threefolding in the Age of the Empire Matrix."
▼ The Walt Disney (or Magic Kingdom) Way—Movement for Recovery and Renewal through The Wonderful Worlds of Disney
▼ Dragon Ball Way (DBW)—Movement for Recovery and Renewal through Akira Toriyama's Dragon Ball World
▼ Hyborian Way—Movement for Recovery and Renewal through Robert E. Howard's Conan Stories
▼ Calvin and Hobbes Way—Movement for Recovery and Renewal through Bill Watterson's Last Great Newspaper Comic
▼ Weirding Way—Movement for Recovery and Renewal through Frank Herbert's Dune Universe
▼ Marvel Way—Movement for Recovery and Renewal through the Marvel Comics Universe. Resource: "America's Comic Book Apocalypse" by anthroposophist Kevin Dann:
   http://realitysandwich.com/100651/america_comic_book_apocalypse
▼ DC Way—Movement for Recovery and Renewal through the DC Comics Universe
▼ Star Trek Way—Movement for Rational Recovery and Renewal through Gene Roddenberry's Star Trek Universe
▼ Time Lord Way—Movement for Recovery and Renewal through the Doctor Who Universe
▼ Way of the Last Best Hope for Peace and Victory—Movement for Recovery and Renewal through J. Michael Straczynski's Babylon 5 Universe
▼ Indiana Jones and the Way of the Twelve Quests—Movement for Recovery and Renewal through George Lucas' Indiana Jones Chronicles. Resource: "The Enduring Legacy of Hans Solo and Indiana Jones" by neo-anthroposophist Douglas Gabriel.
▼ Warcraft Way—Movement for Recovery and Renewal through the World of Warcraft
▼ Dungeons & Dragons Way—Movement for Adventure and Worldbuilding through Gary Gygax's and Dave Arneson's D&D Multiverse (With cover illustration of an adventuring party fighting Lucifer and Mephisto: Dr. S = elven wizard, Marie Steiner = elven bard, Bill W = cleric with triangle-in-circle holy symbol, Dr. Bob = fighter, Lois W = hooded thief? like Sheila, Anne S = ?, Dave Arneson = dwarven fighter, Gygax = dressed like Zagig Ygrane. Asura with purple eyes in darkness of background.)
▼ Dragonlance Way—Movement for Recovery and Renewal through Margaret Weis' & Tracy Hickman's D&D World of Krynn (example of specific world within D&D multiverse)
▼ Humanity: The Way—Movement for Recovery and Renewal through Mark Rein•Hagen's World of Darkness
▼ Tabletop Roleplaying Game Way (encompasses entire history and family tree of TRPGs)

- ▼ Planeswalker Way—Movement for Recovery and Renewal through the Magic: The Gathering Multiverse
- ▼ Ursula K. LeGuin Way (centered on the author and all her works)
- ▼ Earthsea Way (centered on just the Earthsea series)
- ▼ Hainish Cycle Way (centered on all the books of the Hainish series)
- ▼ Odonian Way (centered on just *The Dispossessed* book, which is part of the Hainish Cycle.)
- ▼ Dr. Seuss Way
- ▼ The Way of Pooh—Movement for Recovery and Renewal through A.A. Milne's Hundred Acre Wood
- ▼ Way of the Spark—Movement for Recovery and Renewal through the Transformers Multiverse
- ▼ A Real American Way—Movement for Recovery and Renewal through the G.I. Joe Team
- ▼ Eternia Way—Movement for Recovery and Renewal through He-Man, She-Ra, and the Masters of the Universe
- ▼ Way of Ice and Fire—Movement for Recovery and Renewal through George R. R. Martin's *A Song of Fire & Ice* epic fantasy series
- ▼ The Yellow Brick Way—Movement for Recovery and Renewal through L. Frank Baum's Land of Oz
- ▼ L'Engle Way
- ▼ Wrinkle in Time Way
- ▼ Science Fiction Way (an all-encompassing "lumper" way)
- ▼ Asimov Way (centered on the author and all his works)
- ▼ Foundation Way (just Asimov's Foundation series)
- ▼ Robot Way (just Asimov's Robot series)
- ▼ Fritz Leiber Way
- ▼ Fafhred and the Gray Mouser Way (just that Leiber series)
- ▼ Moorcock Way (all of his works)
- ▼ Eternal Champion Way (just Moorcock's Eternal Champion series)
- ▼ Sherlock Holmes Way
- ▼ Falkner Way
- ▼ Tolstoyan Way
- ▼ Steinbeck Way
- ▼ Hemingway Way
- ▼ Dostoyevskyan Way
- ▼ Dickens Way
- ▼ Anton Chekhov Way
- ▼ Mark Twain Way
- ▼ Nathaniel Hawthorne Way
- ▼ Herman Melville Way
- ▼ Virginia Woolf Way
- ▼ Flannery O'Conner Way
- ▼ James Joyce Way
- ▼ Franz Kafka Way (consulted with Dr. S https://anthropopper.wordpress.com/2014/11/26/franz-kafka-meets-rudolf-steiner/)
- ▼ Aldous Huxley Way (quote about Bill W)
- ▼ John Milton Way / Miltonian Way
- ▼ Manga Way (entire genre)
- ▼ Anime Way (entire genre)
- ▼ Film Way (entire medium)
- ▼ C.S. Lewis Way (all works, not just Narnia)
- ▼ Tolkienian Way (all works, not just Middle-earth)
- ▼ Inklings Way. (Encompasses the works of Tolkien, C.S. Lewis, Charles Williams, Owen Barfield, and others who met at the "Bird & Baby" pub.)
- ▼ Mythopoeic Way (The Inklings, plus all books which have been finalists in the Mythopoeic Awards.)
- ▼ Orson Scott Card Way (based on all his works)
- ▼ Ender's Way—Movement for Recovery and Renewal through Orson Scott Card's *Ender's Game* Universe

Some might wonder how it is possible for the Four Legacies path to be adapted to the lifework of personalities who had serious character flaws, or who denied the spirit. This is how: their Basic Text will tap into the highest potential of that person's soul and work. We frankly note and sift out where certain character traits, views, or deeds are a dead end. For example, the suicidality of Hemingway and Woolf is frankly addressed in the Fifth Quest of the Hemingway Way and Woolf Way. The beer and tobacco in Tolkien's biography and stories are not glossed over in the overview of the First Quest of Middle-earth Way. We frankly lay out how substance use and other afflictions played a role in that soul's life and work, but then we extract the best examples, words, and unrealized intentions from their lifework. What would this persona say if they had worked through the Four Legacies, and thereby deeply connected with Recovery, Humanosophy, and the Threefold Republic? In this way, we clear a path for any lifework or cultural stream to build "higher floors" extending beyond the lower soul world, and thereby reach into the spirit land, where human willingness meets a moral world order. Humane Way seeks to serve as a road-builder and bridge-builder, which facilitates the evolution of countless "cultural soul realms" into becoming pathways which actually extend all the way from the bottom of the U (affliction, jails, institutionalization, and hell on earth), through personal recovery and renewal, and all the way to the outward, millennial kingdom of health, prosperity, and happiness.

Socio-political-, ecological-, scientistic-, and gender/sexuality identity-based ways:
▼ Ethical Individualist Way—Movement for Humanist Recovery and Renewal (intended as the main secular/rationalist/freethinker/agnostic way)
▼ Rainbow Way—Movement for LGBT+ Recovery and Renewal
▼ Woman's Way—Movement for Feminist Recovery and Renewal
▼ Progressive Way—Movement for Liberal and Social Democratic Recovery and Renewal
▼ Libertarian Way—Movement for a Philosophy of Liberty and for a Free Economy, a Free State, and a Free Culture
▼ Marxian Way—Movement for Socialist Recovery and Renewal
▼ Progressive Way—Movement for Recovery and Renewal through Liberal, Social Democracy
▼ Conservative Way—Movement for Recovery and Renewal through Family Values, Fiscal Conservatism, National Tradition, and Faith (see Tea Parties three pillars)
▼ Green Way—Movement for Recovery and Renewal through Social Ecology
▼ Libertarian Way—Movement for a Recovery and Renewal through a Philosophy of Liberty for Free Economy, a Free State, and a Free Culture
▼ Socialist Way—Movement for Recovery and Renewal through Steinerian-Enhanced Socialism
▼ Anarchist Way—Movement for Recovery and Renewal through Benign, Individualist Anarchy
▼ Pirate Way—Movement for Recovery and Renewal through Free Culture
▼ Bioregional Way—Movement for Ecoregional Recovery and Renewal
▼ Social Ecology Way—Movement for Bookchinian Recovery and Renewal
▼ Nature Way—Movement for Ecological Recovery and Renewal (a wide "lumper" way)
▼ Charles Darwin's Way—Movement for Darwinian Recovery and Renewal
▼ Albert Einstein Way (met Dr. S in Prague) https://anthropopper.wordpress.com/2014/11/26/franz-kafka-meets-rudolf-steiner/
▼ United Virtue Way—Movement for Franklinian Recovery and Renewal
▼ Swaraj Way—Movement for Gandhian Recovery and Renewal

Vocation- and lifestyle-centered ways:
▼ Artist's Way, Scientist's Way, Farmer's Way, Actor's Way, Teacher's Way, Doctor's Way, Nurse's Way, Truck Driver's Way, Biker Way (see anthro "Son of Man" club), Hipster Way, Peace Officer's Way
▼ Convenience Store Clerk's Way (personal stories from convenience store clerks worldwide who have traversed through the Four Legacies.)

Fraternal organizations ways:
▼ Freemasonry Way—Movement for Masonic Recovery and Renewal
▼ Rotary Way, Ruritan Way, Lions Club Way, Shriners Way, Oddfellows Way, Fraternal Forestry Way, Woodmen of the World Way, American Legion Way
▼ Scouting Way
▼ various Greek Letter Ways, either for a specific Fraternity/Sorority, for one of the Panhellenic associations, and/or the campus social fraternity/sorority movement as a whole.

Music-based ways: (A few examples, but could be based on any genre, subgenre, band, musician, album, or song.)
- ▼ Conscious Hip-Hop Way, Punk Way, Rock & Roll Way (One resource: Eric Muller's bio book about Rock & Roll.), Rockabilly Way, Funk Way, R&B Way, Classical Music Way, Country Music Way, Outlaw Country Way.

Visual art-based ways: (A few of countless examples, beginning with artists who have a connection with Humane Wisdom.)
- ▼ Beuysian Way
- ▼ Kandinsky Way
- ▼ Piet Mondrian Way
- ▼ Frank Lloyd Wright Way (visited Goetheanum?)

Ways for each of the 12 philosophical worldviews:
- ▼ Materialism Way
- ▼ Spiritism Way
- ▼ Realism Way
- ▼ Idealism Way
- ▼ Mathematism Way
- ▼ Rationalism Way
- ▼ Psychism Way
- ▼ Pneumatism Way
- ▼ Monadism Way
- ▼ Dynamism Way
- ▼ Phenomenalism Way
- ▼ Sensationalism Way

193 civic national ways: (The ones listed here are national cultures which I have witnessed in the Berkshire-Taconic Homeland, via their presence as residents or visitors here. Their basic texts would include quotes and writings from statesmen, folk heroes, and other nationals in the light of the Four Legacies, and would include personal stories of their nationals of all walks of life who have traversed the Four Legacies)
- ▼ American Way—Movement for U.S. National Recovery and Renewal
- ▼ British Way—Movement for U.K. National Recovery and Renewal
- ▼ Nederlandse Weg • Dutch Way—Movement for Netherlandic National Recovery and Renewal
- ▼ Canadian Way • Chemin Canadien—Movement for Canadian National Recovery and Renewal
- ▼ Chemin français • French Way—Movement for Gallic National Recovery and Renewal
- ▼ Derekh Yisra'eli • Israeli Way—Movement for Israeli National Recovery and Renewal
- ▼ Deutsche Weg •German Way—Movement for German National Recovery and Renewal
- ▼ Schweizer Weg • Chemin suisse • Via Svizzera • Via svizra—Movement for Helvetic National Recovery and Renewal
- ▼ Österreichische Weg • Austrian Way
- ▼ Camino Mexicano • Mexican Way
- ▼ Camino Ecuadoriano • Ecuadorian Way
- ▼ Caminho Brasileiro • Brazilian Way
- ▼ Belgische Weg.• Chemin Belge • Belgian Way
- ▼ Via Italiana • Italian Way
- ▼ Camino Dominicana • Dominican Way
- ▼ Ellinikí Odós •Greek Way—Movement for Hellenic National Recovery and Renewal
- ▼ Afghan Way, Australian Way, Bangladeshi Way, Indian Way, Jamaican Way, Japanese Way, Kiwi Way (NZ), Korean Way, Nepalese Way, Russian Way, Trinidadian and Tobagonian Way, Ukrainian Way

Aspirant national ways: (Aspirant nationalities I've witnessed in the Berkshire-Taconic Homeland):
- ▼ Appalachian Way—Movement for Recovery and Renewal through the Highlander Folkways
- ▼ English Way (Episcopal churches here.)
- ▼ Scottish Way (Book about Scottish heritage in Columbia County. Presbyterian churches here.)
- ▼ New Afrikan Way

- ▼ Haudenosaunee Way. (It's a question as to whether there is enough distinction between "nation" and "religion" to inspire two different impulses: Orenda Way and Haudenosaunee Way. But the Orenda Way is pictured as the specifically as a renewal of the Traditional Mysteries, whereas the Haudenosaunee Way includes Haudenosaunee nationals of various sacerdotal traditions: Orenda Mysteries, Handsome Lake Mysteries, and Christian Mysteries.)
- ▼ Mohican Way (Some Mohican Way nationals might also choose to affiliate with the Manitou Way religious path.)
- ▼ Lenape Way (The Oklahoma Lenape still picture the Hudson River basin as part of their traditional territory. Some Lenape nationals might also relate to Manitou Way.)
- ▼ New England Way (Restores the New England Confederation as an independent folk culture.)
- ▼ Rebel (or Confederate) Way—Movement for Southern National Recovery and Renewal (In the Berkshire-Taconic Homeland there is a confederate flag in front of a Claverack house, and on a Philmont truck.)
- ▼ Tibetan Way (Tibetan Buddhist center formerly on Harlemville Road.)
- ▼ Basque Way (Panzur Restaurant in Tivoli. We talked about Mondragon Basque cooperative at local conferences.)

(Two nationalities which have responded to the Threefold Idea):

- ▼ Venda Way. "*Dear Sir/Madam, I wish, on behalf of the Vhavenda people and the DPF, to make a humble submission for the indigenous status of the Vhavenda-Vhangona people and their accompanying* **cultural independence.** *First and foremost we would like to request for formal acknowledgement and recognition of the Vhavenda-Vhangona people as aborigines or natives of the area known as Venda. Secondly we also hereby apply for* **cultural independence in terms of a Trisector model,** *supported by UN Declaration of Indigenous Rights, attached hereto for easy reference. We also refer you to Articles 3, 4, 5 of the Declaration. Respectfully, Makhale T.S {FOR VHAVENDA PEOPLE}*" November 4th, 2011. This is correspondence with the South African government, following my introduction of the Threefold Idea to the Venda indigenous people.
- ▼ Circassian Way. "*Dear Travis Henry, Thank you very much for the information and for giving the Circassian Issue prominence in your very thoughtful scheme, which is very useful to spread amongst the Circassians, and those interested in the Circassian Issue, in the hope that the ideas get stuck and then something is done to implement them in the political sphere. In much appreciation, Amjad Jaimoukha*" Sep 20, 2014.

Note that such Allied Way streams are not the mainline of Humane Way. However, because the WSO is just one Confederated Service Organism among many, each Allied Way is essentially also a World Service Organism. Humane Way is structurally pluri-centric—every place and stream and group is the center. In the further future, or in specific lands, it is possible that one or more Allied Ways might be even more widespread than the "general" Humane Way meetings. That's fine. We still remain united via the World Service Organism. And if some Allied Way develops an iteration of the Four Legacies which is more transformative and acceptable than the general Humane Way, then the entire WSO could very well adopt some or all of these changes. It only takes a ¾ approval from all WSO-registering groups to change the Four Legacies at the world level of service. (In any case, individuals and groups are free to adapt the wording.) In particular, I imagine that the Andréou Hodós (Andrean Way/Eastern Orthodox) Service Organism might be more popular in Russia than ordinary Humane Way, since Russians are a bit allergic to the North American aesthetic.

Noahide Ways: (An Allied Way for each of the 70 Noahide pioneers ("generations of Noah"); with nations grouping themselves according to their traditional Noahide founder. If tradition assigns the nation to two different Noahide pioneers, then the nation belongs to both, meaning that both pioneers played a role. Traditional legends of the fourth son (Strephius/Sceaf), the fifth son (Bouniter/Barvin/Yonton/Maniton, who served the far western continents) and the pioneering daughter (Astgh/"Star", who served the far southern lands, the antipodes) are included. The assignment follows pre-scientist legends (Josephus, Hippolytus, Jerome, Isidore, Rabbincal tradition) rather than DNA or modern scientist critique, since the 3000 BC Noahide event was not so much of a physical-biological or linguistic impulse of migrating peoples, but a civilizational-initiatory impulse of lone pioneers who entered into the multi-lingual human remnants of the global Kali Yuga death-sleep catastrophe. The prevalent nationalistic/racialist interpration of Shem, Japheth, and Ham's assignments as demarcated, mutually-exclusive, militarized territories is a demented, warped view of what would be more clearly perceived as Noahide service areas marked out for the cooperative healing of humanity...of world repair.) To give one example:

- ▼ Magogite Way: Irish, Scots, Goths, Swedes, Finns, Huns, Hungarians, Mongols, and perhaps others.

Anti-Ways: Sick ways which hold sway at present:
- ▼ Alcohol as a Social Lubricant Way
- ▼ Government School Way

- ▼ Entertainment Way / Television Zombie Way / Spectator Sports Way / Virtual Reality Zombie Way / Celebrity Way / Movie Way / Hipster Music Scene Way / Recorded Music Consumer Way / Passive Way
- ▼ Political Circus Way / Liberal versus Conservative Way / Blue State versus Red State Way / Hopeless Partisanship Way
- ▼ Employee Way / Struggle to Make Rent Way
- ▼ Family Lineage Wealth Way / Worshipping a Family Trust Account Way / Family of Origin's Economic-Based Puppeteering Way
- ▼ Servitude to Banks Way / Student Debt + Mortgage Debt Way
- ▼ Consumerist Way / Advertising-Consciousness Way / Corporatist Anti-Culture Way
- ▼ Americanist Way / Corporatist Nation-State Way / Roman-Style Military Tax Tribute Way / National Security Way

Seven prominent Berkshire-Taconic civilizational streams as potential Allied Ways:
From a purely demographic perspective (not considering how it would actually unfold according to individual human whim), besides the mainline Humane Way meetings, the seven priority Allied Ways in the Berkshire-Taconic Homeland might be (listed in alphabetical order):

1. **African-Centered Way** (Black / North American African culture, especially represented in Hudson.)
2. **Bodhi Way** (The Won Buddhist Center is here, along with other Buddhist initiatives and persons.)
3. **Ethical Individualist Way** (Secular/rationalist/skeptic/humanist. Perhaps the most prevalent worldview at this time. This Allied Way would speak only in secular, scientistic, philosophic terms, such as expressed in Dr. S's *Philosophy of Liberty* and *Riddles of Philosophy*.)
4. **Golgothan Way** (or Biblical Way and Petrine Way; much of the populace is nominally Christian, and specifically evangelical or Catholic.)
5. **Sinaïc Way** (Jewish culture has a great presence here and in the rest of the Northeast. Sinaïc Way would clothe the 12 Steps and Anthroposophy in Jewish custom, and vice versa. Its membership would be open to all human beings who are interested in Jewish culture.)
6. **Rainbow Way** (LGBT culture). Important that Humane Way recognize and consolidate the gender question from the start.
7. **Yoga Way** (In recent decades, Yoga practice has made enormous and salutary inroads here and throughout North America.)

*"Then Jesus told them a parable: "Look at the fig tree **and all the trees.** When they sprout leaves, you can see for yourselves and know that summer is near. So also, when you see these things taking place, you will know that the Kingdom of God is near."*

—The Representative of Humanity, speaking in the Gospel of Luke: 21:29
***

the state systems must be replaced throughout the whole world
*"The real impulse of [society] consists in the realization of siblinghood in the widest sense of the term **in the external structure of society.** [...] One must first understand what is meant by siblinghood. On the physical plane **the present state-systems must be replaced throughout the whole world by institutions or organizations which are imbued with siblinghood.**"*

–Dr. S, "From Symptom to Reality in Modern History", Lecture 9 ("brotherhood" is here refreshed as "siblinghood.")

Has anyone conceived or attempted such a comprehensive inner and outer revolution/evolution? Off hand, I know of only five persons in the world, who in modern times have voiced such a goal: three anthroposophists and two other men.

Rudolf Steiner conceived such an external goal, and that is what his final address is about. That is what he hints at in his call for anthroposophists to rise up and salvage human civilization in the 21st Century. Yet he spoke so obliquely, that his words have not easily sunken in. But this is what he is talking about.

Ita Wegman is one who understood what was voiced in-between the lines. Pfeiffer too, from his close friendship with Dr. S, as a protégé. Perhaps other anthroposophists voiced such a concrete, outward vision, but those are the three I know of off-hand.

*"When Rudolf Steiner developed the Threefold Idea (regarding society) it seemed to him to be **the crowning achievement of his lifetime**. He felt that in it **the principles of the Philosophy of Freedom became fruitful for every human being** living with every other human being. Here Rudolf Steiner was least understood. I remember one of the final discussions, which seemed hopeless and fruitless. He walked away from the table and said: 'I think I cannot go on with this work anymore; and I will devote all my time to developing in human beings better thoughts **so that they will be able later better to understand the Threefold Republic.'"[43]**

*"**I would see it as our immediate task to bring about this Threefold Republic first through thought and then through action** [...] **People fool around with things like the United Nations** and don't know how to solve world problems."[44]*

*** *

I know of two other persons in modern times who conceived of a similarly comprehensive path: Benjamin Franklin and Daniel Andreev.

The first is Benjamin Franklin, who, as a 26-year-old young man, conceived a pathway of inner and outer worldwide metamorphosis, which he calls the United Party for Virtue. Five decades later, as a 79 year old, this recollects this unrealized vision in his *Autobiography*:

"Having mentioned a great and extensive project which I had conceived, it seems proper that some account should be here given of that project and its object. Its first rise in my mind appears in the following little paper, accidentally preserved, viz.:

Observations on my reading history, in Library, May 19, 1731.

"That the great affairs of the world, the wars, revolutions, etc., are carried on and effected by parties. [...]

"That few in public affairs act from a mere view of the good of their country, whatever they may pretend; and tho' there actings bring real good to their country, yet men primarily consider that their own and their country's interest was united and did not act from a principle of benevolence.

*"That fewer still, in public affairs, **act with a view to the good of mankind.***

*"There seems to me at present to be great occasion for **raising a United Party for Virtue, by forming the virtuous and good men of all nations into a regular body**, to be governed by suitable good and wise rules, which good and wise men may probably be more unanimous in their obedience to, than common people are to common laws.*
*"I at present think that **whoever attempts this aright, and is well qualified, cannot fail of pleasing God and of meeting with success**. [...]*

*"This is as much as I can now recollect of the project, except that I communicated it in part to two young men, who adopted it with some enthusiasm; but my then narrow circumstances, and the necessity I was under of sticking close to my business, occasioned my postponing the further prosecution of it at that time; and my multifarious occupations, public and private, induced me to continue postponing, so that it has been omitted till I have no longer strength or activity left sufficient for such an enterprise; tho' **I am still of opinion that it was a practicable scheme**, and might have been very useful, by forming a great number of good citizens; and **I was not discouraged by the seeming magnitude of the undertaking**, as I have always thought that **one man of tolerable abilities may work great changes**, and accomplish great affairs among mankind, if he first forms a good plan, and, cutting off all amusements or other employments that would divert his attention, makes the execution of that same plan his sole study and business."*

*** *

The other person is Daniel Andreev, a Russian poet who fully experienced Stalinism. He called such a path, *Roza Mira* "The Rose of the World." I will quote at length from his words—voiced during a ten-year sojourn in a labor camp—which ring out to each subsequent generation of humanity...

---

[43] p.6, Lecture 1, August 1, 1947, given at Threefold Farm in Spring Valley, N.Y., printed in *Rudolf Steiner: Two Lectures by E.E. Pfeiffer*, Vulcan Books, Spring Valley?, 1979?

[44] pp.41-42, Lecture 5, December 22, 1946, *The Task of the Archangel Michaël*, by Ehrenfried Pfeiffer, Mercury Press, 1985.

"Perhaps the worst will never come to pass and tyranny on such a scale will never recur. Perhaps humanity will forevermore retain the memory of Russia's terrible historical experience. [...]

"But I number among those who have been fatally wounded by two great calamities: world war and dictatorship. [...] For me and others like me, both those calamities were a kind of apocalypse—revelations of the power of planetary Evil and of its age-old struggle with the forces of Light. Those living in other times would probably not understand us.

"I am seriously ill—my days are numbered. If this manuscript is destroyed or lost, I will not be able to rewrite it in time. But if, sometime in the future, it reaches only a few persons whose spiritual thirst drives them to surmount all its difficulties and read it through to the end, then the idea planted within cannot help but become seeds that will sprout in their hearts. [...]

"This book is directed, first and foremost, against the two basic, supreme evils of war and dictatorship. It is directed against them not as a simple warning, nor as a satire that unmasks their true nature, nor as a sermon. [...] They are useless if they are not based on a worldview, global teaching, and program of action that, spread from mind to mind and will to will, would be capable of averting these evils. [...]

"This is a book that, if God saves it from destruction, will be laid, as one of many bricks, in the foundation of the Rose of the World, at the base of a Community of all humanity.[...]

"Now American cosmopolitanism is occupied with avoiding the mistakes of its predecessors. [...]

"We must, rather, recognize the absolute necessity of the one and only path: the establishment, over a global federation of states, of an unsullied, incorruptible, highly respected body, a moral [cultural] body standing outside of and above the state. [...] [Note: In the Threefold Republic, the cultural organism stands outside of, but beside the human rights state –TH]

"What idea, what teaching will aid in the creation of such a body? What minds will formulate its guiding principles and make it acceptable to the overwhelming majority of people? By what paths will such a body—a body foreswearing the use of force—arrive at worldwide recognition, at a position higher than a federation of states? If it can in fact introduce something into leadership the policy of [...] replacing coercion with something else, then what would that something else be? And in what manner would it be introduced? And what doctrine would be able to solve the incredibly complex problems that will arise in connection with all that? [...]

"One need not assume that such a process will require enormous spans of time. [...] Nazi Germany, for example, managed to achieve its goals in this area in the span of a single generation. Clearly its ideals can elicit no response in us other than anger and disgust. Its methods, as well, must be rejected almost wholesale. But we must take hold of the lever it discovered and not let go. The century of mass spiritual enlightenment, the century of decisive victories for a new, as yet barely discernable pedagogy is approaching. Even if only a few dozen schools are operating on its principles, a generation capable of doing its duty out of free will, not coercion, a generation acting out of creative impulses and love, not fear, would form there. That is the essence of an <u>ennobling education</u>.

"I picture an international organization, both political and cultural in nature, setting as its aim the transformation of the state through the consistent implementation of far-reaching reforms. The crucial stage in the fulfillment of that aim will be the foundation of the Global Federation of Independent States. [What I call the Humane States Organism. TH] But this must carry the proviso that a special body be established over the Federation—the body I have already mentioned [...] [In trisecting terms, this would be the Humane Cultures Organism, not above the Humane States Organism, but as an independent peer. The third peer is the Humane Economies Organism.]

"I consider it both premature and unnecessary to speculate on the structure and name of that organization. For now [...] we will give it a provisional name: the League for the Transformation of the State. {This is what I call Threefold Now: Movement for the Differentiation of the Economy, State, and Culture. Threefold Now is a Humane Way-inspired league for the triform transformation of the State. -TH] As for its structure, those who will be its founders will be both more experienced and more practical than I— they will be leaders of vision, not poets. I will only say that it seems to me *personally that the League should establish branches in every country, with each branch consisting of several divisions: cultural, philanthropic [economic], educational, and political. [...]*

"How, where, and among whom specifically the formation of the League will take place, I, of course, do not and cannot know. But it is clear that the period of time from its inception until the establishment of the Federation of States [the Humane States -TH] and the moral supervisory body [the Cultural Council] over it [alongside it] will be regarded as a preliminary stage, when the League will channel all of its energies into dissemination its ideas, recruiting new members, expanding its operations, educating younger generations ,and forging within itself a future body that in time can be entrusted with a global leadership role.

The League's composition will not restrict its membership to people of any particular philosophical or religious belief. All that will be required is an active commitment to realizing its program and a resolve not to violate its moral code, the cornerstone of the organization.

"Despite all the vicissitudes of public service, the goals of the League must be obtained not at the prices of departure from its moral code but as a result of faithful adherence to it. [...] The best and finest of humanity will be drawn to it and will constantly strengthen its ranks.

"Oh, there will of course be many people who will insist that the League's methods are impractical and unrealistic. I've met enough champions of political realism to last me a lifetime. [...] Such political realists are, incidentally, the same sort of people who in their time claimed, even in India, that Gandhi was a dreamer out of touch with reality. [...]

"People's spiritual thirst will become unbearable. The elimination of the threat of great wars, the discovery of paths to uniting the world without bloodshed, a spiritual leader and living saint who will head a united humanity in the future [That rules me out, since I'm not a saint But I am alive! –TH], the weakening of state coercion, and the growth of a global community spirit—this is what believers pray for and nonbelievers dream about in our century. [...]

"No one but God knows where and when the Rose of the World's first flames will be kindled. The country—Russia—has been designated; tragic events might still take place that could interfere with that mystical event and force it to be relocated to another country. [...] It is possible that the first flame will kindle in a different, as yet unknown group of people."

"But here or there, in this country or another, a decade earlier or later, the interreligious global church of the new age—the Rose of the World—will appear as the sum total of the spiritual activity of many people, as the joint creation of people standing beneath the shower of heaven-sent revelation—it will appear, emerge, and embark on its historical journey.

"Religion, interreligion, church—I cannot render the idea with necessary exactitude using those words. [...] It will not be like any restricted religious faith, whether true or false. Nor will it be an international religious order like the Theosophists, Anthroposophists, or the Masons, composed, like a bouquet, of various flowers of truth eclectically picked from every imaginable religious glade. It will be an interreligion or pan-religion, in that it will be a teaching that views all religions that appeared earlier as reflections of different layers of spiritual reality, different sets of variomaterial facts, and different segments of our planetary cosmos. [...] If the older religions are petals, the Rose of the World will be a flower: with roots, stem, head, and the commonwealth of its petals. [...]

"From that follows [...] a program of consistent, spiritual-historical tasks that are entirely concrete and achievable in principle. I will list once again the foremost of them: the unification of the planet under a federation of states overseen by a moral [cultural] supervisory body; the establishment of economic well-being and a high standard of living in every country; the ennobling education of younger generations; the reunification of the Christian churches and the creation of a free amalgamation of all religions of Light; the transformation of the planet into a garden and the state into a community. But those are merely tasks of the first order. Their realization will open the way to tasks of an even higher order [...]

"Revelation flows down from many streams, and if art is not the purest then it is at least the widest of them. Therefore, every art form and a beautiful repertoire of ritual will outfit the Rose of the World with colorful and glittering habiliments. And for that same reason, it would be most natural for a person who possesses three of the greatest gifts—religious vision,

sanctity, and artistic genius—to stand at the head of the Rose of the World. [Shucks, that rules me out again. However, I still aim to clear a pathway for aftercomers who bear the gracefulness to serve as a better pied piper than I. -TH]

"Perhaps such a person will never come, or will come much later. It is possible that a collective of the worthiest, and not one single person, will lead the Rose of the World. [Humane Way intends for 4x12 leaders. –TH] *But if Providence sends a person of such great spirit to our century—and it has sent them before—and the forces of evil are unable to thwart his or her mission, it will be the greatest of good fortune for the entire planet. [...]*

"Some will say that such people appear perhaps only once in every five-hundred years. I will go one step further: individuals of such stature, who possess the sum of these above-mentioned gifts, could never have existed before. [...]

"Not a hierocracy, not a monarchy, not an oligarchy, not a republic: something qualitatively different from all that has come before will emerge."

—Daniel Andreev, *The Rose of the World*
Written in prison during the 1950s and completed in 1958, the year before his death.

Humane Way is, or is intended d to be, the Rose of the World. Humane Way's political branch—provisionally named "Threefold Now"—is the League for the Transformation of the State.

***

My perception differs from Andreev in several regards, but it was a relief when I read his text earlier this year, to know of one other humane being with the audacity to conceive and voice such a path. There may be others, perhaps several others, who have conceived such a comprehensive revolution/evolution, but those are five: Franklin, Steiner, Wegman, Pfeiffer, and Andreev.

None of them actually did it though. Of course they all made great, preparatory efforts, such as Franklin's role in the establishment of the Democratic Republic, and the anthroposophists' first effort for the Threefold Republic from 1917 to 1922.

Will I continue all the way to Humane Way's fruition? Who knows? I might give up tomorrow and retire, delve into my hobbies, or raise a family. But there is a lawfulness in my intentions and actions which has steadily unfolded since 2009, when I shared my first hand-drawn images of a Threefold World, in a church basement in Chicago. That was seven years ago. I do strive one day at a time, in day-sized compartments.

*"A task is still awaiting fulfilment: the seeking the treading of the path to the spiritual world **and the forming of humanity into a true and worthy social body over the whole earth.** Michaël's aim is to bring about that true knowledge and understanding of Christ which, **living itself out in moral action**, leads the individual to freedom **and the world in its totality to harmony."***

—Ita Wegman, "On the Work of the Archangel Michaël", 1930
***

the threefold republic as the twelfth quest

Unlike in Anthroposophy-as-it-exists, the Threefold Republic cannot be separated from the Humane Way spiritual path.

Wherever there are Wayfarers who have passed through the Twelfth Quest, there is a symbolic Threefold Republic. We are the Threefold Republic. Because in Humane Way, the only level of sovereignty is the Home Group and the Individual, each local group—to the extent it has members who have traversed the Twelfth Quest—will have an initiated a local Threefold Republic Project with a service area which is meaningful to their local group or groups, for example:

- ▼ The Threefold Republic in the Berkshire-Taconic Region
- ▼ The Threefold Republic in Chestnut Ridge/Spring Valley, New York
- ▼ The Threefold Republic in the Driftless Area
- ▼ The Threefold Republic in Southeastern Pennsylvania

Such Threefold Republics are modeled on the Free State Project in New Hampshire, as a fast, free, and fun way of living into the idea. Each Threefold Republic delineates a symbolic service area on the map, as a Threefold Homeland. Each Threefold Republic adopts its own symbology. We cultivate a grounded sense of place. Because service areas can overlap, it's okay for there to be instances where Threefold Republic Projects overlap with each other.

Every outer political jurisdiction which is included within (or partially overlapped by) a Threefold group's service area is symbolically trisected too. For example, within the Threefold Republic in the Berkshire-Taconic Region, our initiative would begin to conceive of trisecting each of the incorporated Villages, Towns, and Cities within our Homeland: Threefold Philmont, Threefold Ghent, Threefold Hillsdale, Threefold Austerlitz, Threefold Copake, Threefold Claverack, Threefold Hudson, Threefold Egremont, Threefold Great Barrington, and so forth. But also the counties, states/provinces, and nation-states which overlap with our nascent republic: a Threefold County of Columbia and Threefold County of Berkshire, a Threefold State of New York and Threefold Commonwealth of Massachusetts...and the Threefold States (United States). We begin to at least symbolically trisect whatever lies within our spiritual-geographic membrane.

Another example, a Threefold Republic Project in the Driftless Area would begin to conceive and spawn not only a Threefold Wisconsin, but also a Threefold Illinois, Threefold Iowa, Threefold South Dakota, and Threefold Minnesota, since the Driftless Area straddles the corner of four states.

The threefold flags I have designed for each country and state/province are actually put to use as symbols of our trisected model, parallel, symbolic (but not *merely* symbolic) version of those external states. Though of course a revised or different design could be adopted by any group according to their own aesthetic.

We also form our own Model Trisecting Societies (M3S) clubs as a parallel of the Model United Nations (MUN) clubs. Our M3S use the Threefold UN flags which have been designed by Threefold Now.

 Welcome to the Trisected Societies. This is humanity's world.
We, the cultures, democracies, and economies...
A wiser, more loving, and stronger 3S for the best possible world.

The Trisected Societies Organism (3SO)

(Threefolding the United Nations System)

The Humane Economies
(HE)

humanity's economic headquarters:
Fraternity Tower/
Threefold World Trade Center
(3 WTC),
New York City

"*Their violent and instant demise, together with its catastrophic loss of life, was a tragedy that belongs not to a single nation, but to the world. The challenge to decipher meaning from this tragedy was placed by world destiny before every human being, so that good might arise out of their fall.*" —Gisela Wielki

The Humane States
(HS)

humanity's political-rights headquarters:
Sarajevo, Bosnia

The Humane Cultures
(HC)

humanity's cultural headquarters:
Jerusalem
The global seat of the plurinational cultural councils.

The linden, olive, and wheat represent Liberty, Equality, and Fraternity.
The three map emblems were projected for Threefold Now by cartographer daan Strebe.

Though not visible in this black-and-white edition, the cultural flag is rose red with golden highlights, the rights flag is gold, and the economic flag is chicory (or cornflower) blue with wheat-colored highlights.

the golden path

How it works:

Anyone who reads this is welcome to come with me.

Since July of 2014, I have traversed the Twelve Steps, and the first five Quests. I am on the cusp of the Sixth Quest. Though it has taken me two years to trudge this far, others might be able to move through their adventures more quickly.

I'm aiming to write a Provisional Basic Text of Humane Way later this summer and fall. It is an action-based guidebook to the 4x12 adventures.

Sometime in the coming months, there will be the first trial meeting of Humane Way. It will be an opportunity to get feedback on the meeting format.

The Fellowship of Humane Way does not exist until there are two Wayfarers.

I have spoken with AA's World Service Office, and AA is prepared to grant permission to adapt the Three Legacies of AA into an anthroposophic framework.

When there is another person who has worked through the Steps and Quests in the context of Humane Way, the provisional wording of the Steps and Quests is changed from "I" to "we."

When there are two or more of us who have enacted all 180 Actions, then a World Service Body is formed.

The wording of the Four Legacies would be affirmed by 2 or more persons, and then the Four Legacies would be submitted to AA World Service in order to finalize the permission to adapt AA's Three Legacies.

The World Service Body is intend to grow to 48 members; 4x12 Wayfarers who have done the 180 Actions.

Other Wayfarers' experience and feedback will inform the next revision of the Provisional Basic Text. And their (anonymized) personal story could be added to the text. The WSB will revise and approve a collectively-authored Basic Text, so that it is no longer provisional.

At a certain point, we begin propagating the message. We put up a public website, and post notices in anthroposophical and recovery forums, newsletters, and magazines.

Twelve Step fellowships tend to grow and grow.

In the year when Humane Way membership surpasses the number of members in the General Anthroposophical Society (at this point, reportedly 60,000 worldwide), we invite the Society to fully converge with Humane Way. That is the act of recognition we seek from the Leadership of the Goetheanum in Dornach.

***

Do any of you have a better plan for realizing Dr. S's dying wish for 4x12 leaders to arise? If so, then show me. If not, *then won't you join me?*

Made in the USA
Las Vegas, NV
16 November 2020